A GUIDE
TO USABILITY

HUMAN FACTORS IN COMPUTING

EDITED BY
Jenny Preece

David Benyon, Gordon Davies, Laurie Keller, Jenny Preece and Yvonne Rogers

ADDISON-WESLEY

Wokingham, England · Reading, Massachusetts · Menlo Park, California · New York
Don Mills, Ontario · Amsterdam · Bonn · Sydney · Singapore · Tokyo · Madrid · San Juan
Milan · Paris · Mexico City · Seoul · Taipei

The Open
University

D0490942

PREECE/A Guide to Usability

Most of the material in this Guide was derived from a course on Human–Computer Interaction (HCI) that was produced by the Open University. Funding from the Department of Trade and Industry (DTI) 'Usability Now Programme' enabled us to distil the contents of the course, add some additonal material and produce an earlier version of this text. The original *Guide to Usability* was distributed by the DTI via the HCI Centres to those attending special seminars and meetings arranged as part of the Usability Now Programme. Due to the large number of requests for copies that have been received by the Open University, we have revised the Guide and published it as a book so that it is easily available for those who want copies.

We should like to thank the DTI for funding the development of the original Guide and also for their helpful comments on early drafts. We should also like to acknowledge the contribution of the Course Team and consultants who developed the Open University HCI course. If you would like to know more about this course you should contact the Open University Customer Services Department (0908 653917).

Edited, designed and typeset by The Open University
Cover designed by Designers and Partners of Oxford
and printed by The Riverside Printing Co. (Reading) Ltd.
Printed in Great Britain by William Clowes, Beccles, Suffolk.

ISBN 0-201-62768-X

First printed 1993.

British Library Cataloguing in Publication Data
A catalogue record for this book is available from the British Library.

More and more people use and depend on information technology (IT). Be it the point-of-sale system in a supermarket, the automatic cash dispenser in a bank, the control system in a cockpit or the word processor in an office – all have become an integral and indispensable part of life. A big problem with this change is that *most* of us at some time or other have experienced frustration and difficulty when trying to *use* the technology. Much time and energy – and in some cases lives – have been lost in this struggle.

To overcome this problem in the future we need to design systems that take into account the people who are to use them and the way they are to be used. In particular, we need to develop new technology that is both *usable* and *effective*. This means designing for health, safety, efficiency and even enjoyment!

Human–computer interaction (or HCI) is a rapidly developing field which considers problems related to the *usability* of systems. This Guide is intended to help you to understand the importance of HCI. It outlines ways in which to specify and design more usable systems. Most importantly, it will help you to understand the role of users and the best ways in which to design computer systems that match users' needs.

Example

Suppose your company's existing computer equipment is under-used. Many of the office staff have complained that it is old-fashioned, far too cumbersome and unreliable. In addition, you have never made much use of the expensive workstation that was bought to help you with project management. You decide it is time to revamp the whole company with state-of-the-art computer technology with the purpose of improving productivity and staff morale. How do you go about it?

After reading through this Guide the main factors that need to be considered should become clear to you. These include:

- what the users' needs are
- what types of software and hardware are most suited to your environment
- how the organization should be restructured to make the transition from where you are now to where you want to be as smooth as possible
- how to evaluate its effectiveness.

The important thing is to find out, *right from the start*, what the users need to carry out their work.

Who is this Guide for?

This Guide is intended primarily for technical managers, system designers, and anyone who is responsible for the specification, development and implementation of IT. Practitioners, programmers, product designers and general managers may also find it a valuable source of reference.

Students of introductory courses in human–computer interaction may also find this text useful because it contains a broad and very condensed overview of the subject with suggested further reading for those who want to know more. It will also be of interest to students of Business, Accountancy and Computing at HND or first-year University level and is suitable for use as introductory material to MSc Computing conversion courses.

How to use this Guide

This Guide is organized around the concept of a wheel. There are eight sections: the hub and seven spokes. The figure opposite presents an overall map of the Guide. Each spoke is a major area that needs to be considered in the design of computer systems. The hub, Chapter 1 Introduction to HCI, is concerned with the major issues in HCI, the key terms, its importance and role and its contributors. *If you read nothing else read Chapter 1.*

Branching out from the hub are the spokes. The top spoke, Chapter 2 The Human Element, highlights the limits of what people can be expected to do given their psychological capabilities. It also pinpoints the thorny issues surrounding the way people work together. In particular, this spoke explains some of the factors that can make the introduction of computer systems in an organization either a failure or success.

The next four spokes going clockwise round the wheel (Chapters 3 to 6) cover most of the important information that is needed to *design* effective, easy-to-use and safe systems. They cover the design process and various software tools, design techniques, and evaluation methods that are part of good HCI design. The last spoke, Chapter 7 Future Trends, provides a flavour of what is likely to happen in the future.

At the beginning of each chapter the hub or spoke is expanded to show in more detail the contents of that chapter. A Glossary of terms, References and Further Reading, and an Index are provided at the end of the Guide.

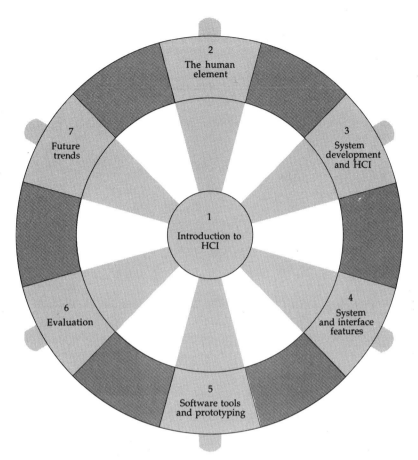

Overall structure of the Guide

Example

Suppose you are thinking of introducing voice input and output in a stock control system. What considerations would you need to think about?

You should first read about speech input/output devices in Sections 4.1 and 4.2, and then move to Chapter 2 to see what psychological issues to take into account. Once you have appreciated the nature of the problem, you should go on to read about system development in Chapter 3 and assessing its potential effectiveness in Chapter 6.

This Guide introduces good practice in usability and the important issues that need to be addressed. It is not intended to provide all the answers or teach you new principles and techniques but to point you in the right direction. References to information cited in the text and suggested further reading are listed on pages 132 to 136 so that you can consult them for further details if necessary. Articles or books that are either very easy to read or highly technical are coded accordingly.

Human–computer interaction (HCI) is concerned with the design of computer systems that are safe, efficient, easy and enjoyable to use as well as functional.

Other names that are virtually synonymous with human–computer interaction include 'man–machine interaction' (MMI) and 'user–system interaction' (USI).

1.1   What is HCI?

'What is neither animal, vegetable nor mineral yet is as important to the operation of modern industrial society as oil and coal? What is colourless, odourless, tasteless, intangible – yet is a substance manipulated, processed, packaged and sold by over sixty percent of the British workforce?'

The answer to both these questions is information.
(APEX, 1979)

Information manifests itself in many forms: digits on a computer, words on a screen, sounds, pictures, codes, blips on an air traffic controller's screen, grooves in a record, and so on. IT is about processing and transferring information using technology, particularly computers. The number of people involved in this activity has increased dramatically during the last decade and continues to do so. Consequently, computer systems are used by a wide range of people for all kinds of purposes.

HCI studies are concerned with understanding how people use computer systems so that better systems can be designed which more closely meet users' needs.

The knowledge necessary for this comes from understanding how users interact with computer systems in particular work environments. This interaction consists of four components:

- the *user*
- who has to do a particular *task* or *job*
- in a particular *context*
- using a *computer system*.

These four components are represented in Figure 1.1.

Figure 1.1   The interaction between a user and a computer system

Each of these four components has its own characteristics, all of which influence the nature of the interaction between the user and the computer system (Section 1.3) or, as is becoming increasingly common, between several users and one or more software applications. Regardless of the kind of task that a user wants to do (for example, correct a letter, monitor a chemical reaction, obtain sales statistics) it will need to be broken down into small units (subtasks) which relate to the dialogue used for communicating with the computer system. This communication involves very small subtasks which have been through many decompositions.

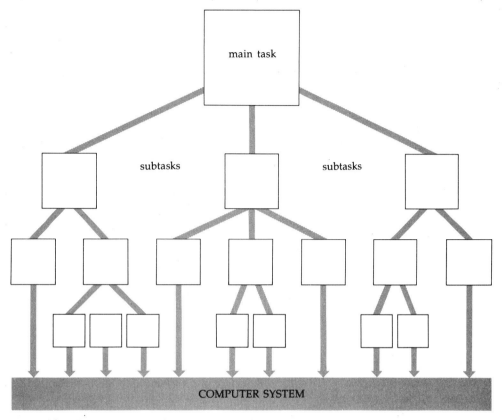

Figure 1.2   Decomposing a task

The user interface of a computer system is the medium through which a user communicates with the computer. The form of this interface has a strong influence on how a user views and understands the functionality of a system. Consequently, the user interface can be thought of as those aspects of the system with which the user comes into contact both physically and cognitively.

Figure 1.3   An example of a user interface (the user has to tell the computer system what to write and under which name)

The user interface has a specific form of dialogue which is designed to facilitate user–computer interaction. This dialogue enables the user to map (or relate) the details of tasks to the functionality of the computer system.

A well-designed user interface makes it easy and natural for a user to break down (or decompose) a task into subtasks and map them on to the system's functions. A poorly-designed computer system requires its user to decompose tasks in unnatural ways and the ensuing mapping is then prone to errors.

An important part of HCI work therefore involves understanding the nature of users' tasks and the ways in which users most naturally decompose them. This in turn requires understanding the characteristics of users themselves and the influence on their behaviour of the context in which they work. In addition, designers have to take into account technical and logistic considerations.

1.2   Why HCI is important

The goals of HCI are to develop and improve systems that include computers so that users can carry out their tasks:

- safely (especially in critical systems like air traffic control)
- effectively
- efficiently, and
- enjoyably.

These aspects are collectively known as usability.

'And I bought this one to explain the manual of the first one.'

Well-designed computer systems with good usability can:

- improve the performance of the workforce
- improve the quality of life
- make the world a safer and more enjoyable place to live in.

While it is sometimes difficult to see the effects of good interface design, there are, unfortunately, many examples of the effects of poor interface design.

Example

The results of the Three Mile Island nuclear power plant disaster revealed, amongst other things, that displays and controls were located in such a way that some were obscured by others. In addition, there were conflicting messages from feedback and other problems which prevented the operators from understanding what was happening and reacting quickly in the proper manner. The result was a life-threatening situation and an expensive disaster.

As well as endangering life, poor interface design can result in loss of money (often a lot!). Shackel (1990) provides case studies to illustrate this point.

1.3 The scope of HCI

Designing usable systems requires knowledge about:

- who will use the system
- what it will be used for
- the work context and environment in which it will be used
- what is technically and logistically feasible.

Users

Designers need knowledge of the physiological and psychological capabilities (Section 2.2) of users in order to design appropriate systems.

Darn these hooves! I hit the wrong switch again! Who designs these instrument panels, raccoons?

It is also important to realize that users are not a homogenous group of people. They differ from each other in the following ways:

- physically, in terms of height, weight, reach, left- or right-handedness, dexterity, visual acuity, general health and fitness, and so on
- in their experience and knowledge of the task they want to do and of computer systems
- psychologically: they may be adventurous or timid, learn fast or slowly, have good memories or bad memories
- socio-culturally, in terms of background, educational attainment, age, gender, race and ethnic background.

Any or all of the above factors can influence how an individual will cope with using a computer system.

Example

Deciding upon colour coding can be fraught with difficulty (aside from the problem of colour-blindness) because of the 'cultural' meanings of colour: to a physicist blue may signify 'cold', whereas to a geographer it means 'a body of water'; red means 'stop' or 'danger' but it can also mean 'warm' or 'hot', denote a political persuasion or simply be used to code a group of items in contrast to other items.

Tasks

Tasks vary greatly and a wide range have now become automated. These include:

- office tasks (for example, producing reports)
- engineering tasks (for example, cutting out patterns)
- information retrieval tasks (for example, obtaining information on the quality of a product)
- transaction tasks (for example, banking, reservations)
- control tasks of various types (for example, controlling chemical flow).

In many cases computers have largely automated manual tasks, but in others they have introduced new flexibility.

*'You're right. It **is** a great wine!'*

Computers have even made possible undertakings that could not have been done without them, for example, simulating the effects of global warming and forecasting long-term economic trends.

The characteristics of tasks that designers need to consider include:

- whether the task is repetitive and is affected very little by changes in the environment
- to what extent the task varies from one occasion to the next
- whether the task will be carried out regularly, infrequently or only once
- what kinds of skills and knowledge are required to perform the task
- whether time is critical
- whether there are safety hazards
- whether the wearing of protective clothing by a user is necessary or whether other unusual conditions apply (for example, the existence of a disability in the user) which might require specialist input and output devices
- whether the user will do the task alone or with others
- whether the user will normally be switching between this and several other tasks.

Work context and environment

Every organization has a culture of its own. It has ways of working, ways of socializing, 'office' or 'shop-floor' politics, written and unwritten rules about behaviour, and so on. The advent of a computer system, or a change to an existing computer system, can change the culture in unforeseen ways. This is particularly the case with systems that encourage collaborative working or switching between two or more tasks (multi-tasking).

Some aspects that may be affected by computer systems are:

- job content, including who does what, how much is done, what way it is done (computers tend to make things more, not less, formal), who is trained when and how, whether the alteration affects pay, conditions and job satisfaction

- power and influence (this may shift between individuals, or between formal groups such as departments, or between informal groups)

- personnel policies, which will probably have to change as a result, at least, of the changes in job content.

In addition, the physical conditions in which the work is done must be considered. Poor lighting, for example, may make visual display of information unsuitable or undesirable. Health and safety also are important.

Examples

Two health and safety aspects of computer use widely talked about are:

- the possibility of low-level radiation from visual display units causing harm to pregnant women, and its possible association with eye-strain and headaches

- repetitive strain injury (RSI) caused by poorly designed furniture and equipment that require an unnatural posture and result in strain.

More about the work environment appears in Section 2.3.

The constraints of the system

As well as deciding what would be ideal from the point of view of users, their tasks and their work environment, designers and HCI specialists have to work within technical and logistic constraints. Technical constraints include memory size and availability of compatible input and output devices. Logistic constraints relate to factors such as costs, schedules, staffing and pressures from the company to, say, increase productivity or decrease production costs.

Interaction between factors

One of the most important considerations when solving an HCI problem is to identify and discriminate among the many factors involved. The way that these factors inter-relate can be complex. Figure 1.4 classifies the main user, task and context factors and identifies a number of technical aspects and constraints.

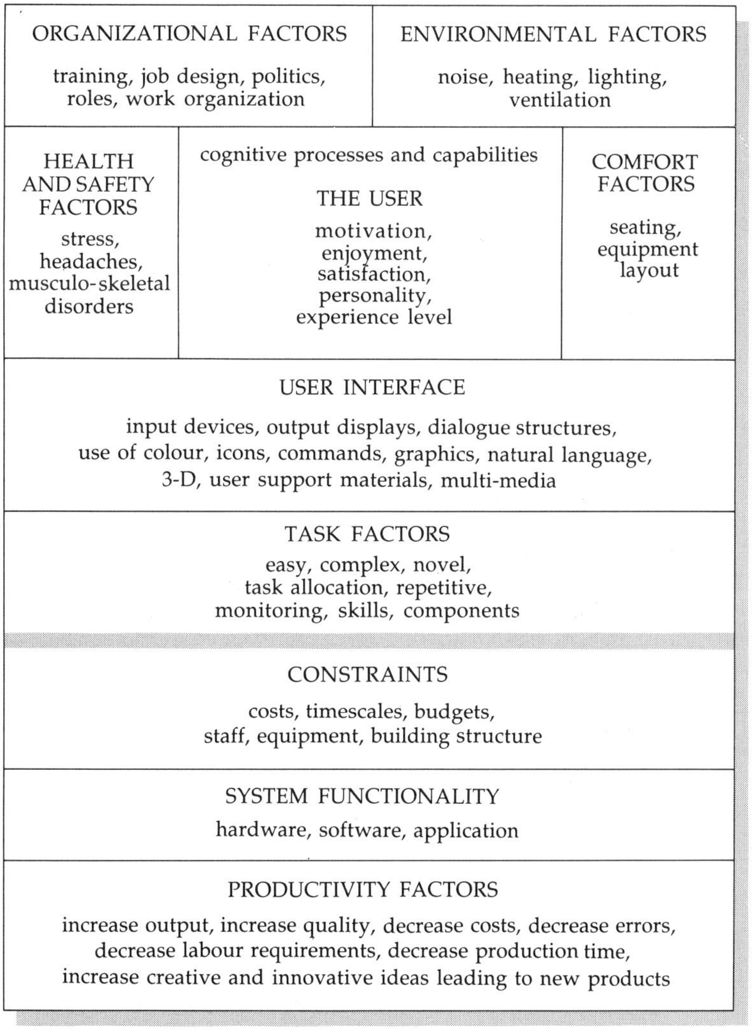

ORGANIZATIONAL FACTORS	ENVIRONMENTAL FACTORS
training, job design, politics, roles, work organization	noise, heating, lighting, ventilation

HEALTH AND SAFETY FACTORS	cognitive processes and capabilities	COMFORT FACTORS
stress, headaches, musculo-skeletal disorders	THE USER motivation, enjoyment, satisfaction, personality, experience level	seating, equipment layout

USER INTERFACE
input devices, output displays, dialogue structures, use of colour, icons, commands, graphics, natural language, 3-D, user support materials, multi-media

TASK FACTORS
easy, complex, novel, task allocation, repetitive, monitoring, skills, components

CONSTRAINTS
costs, timescales, budgets, staff, equipment, building structure

SYSTEM FUNCTIONALITY
hardware, software, application

PRODUCTIVITY FACTORS
increase output, increase quality, decrease costs, decrease errors, decrease labour requirements, decrease production time, increase creative and innovative ideas leading to new products

Figure 1.4   Factors to be considered in HCI

1.4   The contributors to HCI

HCI is a multi-disciplinary field; the main areas that contribute to it are shown in Figure 1.5.

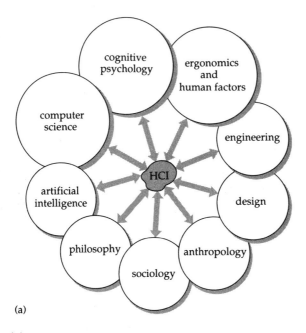

(a)

Figure 1.5   Disciplines that contribute to HCI

The main contributions come from computer science, cognitive psychology, ergonomics (a European term) and its sister discipline human factors (an American term). Other areas of interest are artificial intelligence, philosophy, sociology, anthropology, design and engineering.

Human beings are highly variable: they are often subject to lapses of concentration, changes in mood, motivation and emotion, have prejudices and fears, make errors and misjudgements, and so on. On the other hand, they are capable of remarkable feats: they can perceive and respond rapidly to external stimuli, solve complex problems, create masterpieces. Many system designers, however, have paid only scant attention to this 'human element'. Users are simply regarded as being another part of the data transformation process. The assumption is that the user will fit in with the system like a cog in a machine. However, as many of you will have experienced, such systems are often very difficult to use and can cause errors.

It is important that future systems be designed which make the human element a central concern. To achieve this we need to begin by applying psychology (our understanding of the way people act and react in their environment) to a design or implementation problem.

'You're suffering from sensory overload. Cut down on your intake of media.'
Drawing by Koren; © 1967 The New Yorker Magazine, Inc.

2.1   Why apply psychology?

When people interact with a computer system they are primarily interacting with *information*. Their objective in using the machine is to carry out a task in which information is accessed, manipulated or created. The computer and peripheral devices are the means through which this objective is achieved. To this end human–computer interaction is essentially *cognitive*, that is, it involves the processing of information in the mind. The overall aim of applying cognitive psychology to system design is therefore to ensure that this information processing activity is within the capabilities of the users' mental processes.

Cognitive psychology can help to improve the design of computer systems by:

- providing knowledge about what users can and cannot be expected to do
- identifying and explaining the nature and causes of the problems users encounter
- supplying modelling tools to help build more compatible interfaces.

In most cases computer systems are used not in isolation but within an organization. In order to maximize their use when introduced into everyday work environments it is also necessary to apply *organizational* and *social psychology*.

Organizational and social psychology can help when introducing new computer systems into the workplace by:

- providing knowledge about the structure and working practices of businesses and institutions
- identifying and explaining any problems resulting from changes to work practices
- giving a better understanding of the social aspects (such as attitudes) of computer use and implementation
- suggesting methods by which to restructure an organization with the aim of improving the quality of working life.

2.2   What is cognitive psychology?

To understand how to apply psychology it is important initially to understand what is relevant to HCI. This section considers the key areas of cognitive psychology which underlie the way people interact with systems. These are perception, attention, information processing, memory, learning and mental models.

Visual perception

The process of seeing is an active process. When we see things we do not see a replica of the external world but a model of it constructed by our visual system. Both information from the environment and previously stored knowledge are

used. The effect is to provide us with a more constant view of the world than if we were merely to 'see' the flux of unstable images that are projected on to our retinas. During this process sensory input and information are organized. The main organization is the separation of the 'figure', the object of interest and focus, from the 'background'. This enables us to distinguish objects from the surrounding background. In addition, visual depth cues enable us to perceive the world as three-dimensional. The application of these cues is what also enables us to perceive three-dimensional objects in two-dimensional representations (such as pictures, photographs, films). These cues are used to make computer graphics more realistic. (For more on the application of perception see Schiff, 1980.)

Computer systems can display information in a number of ways: as text, graphics, animation, video or combinations of these. When designing screen displays it is important to ensure that the information is:

- legible (the text does not flicker and is easy to read at a glance)
- distinguishable (the figure is clearly separated from the background)
- comprehensible
- uncluttered (see example below)
- meaningfully structured (see example below).

For more about the specifics of screen design see Section 4.3.

Example

Figure 2.1 shows two different screen displays. See how long it takes you to find the phone number of Howard Johnsons in Columbia in part (a) and the phone number of Holiday House in part (b).

City	Motel/Hotel	Area Code	Phone	Rates Single	Double
Charleston	Best Western	883	747-8961	$26	$38
Charleston	Days Inn	883	881-1888	$18	$24
Charleston	Holiday Inn N	883	744-1621	$36	$46
Charleston	Holiday Inn SW	883	556-7188	$33	$47
Charleston	Howard Johnsons	883	524-4140	$31	$36
Charleston	Ramada Inn	883	774-8281	$33	$48
Charleston	Sheraton Inn	883	744-2401	$34	$42
Columbia	Best Western	883	796-9400	$29	$34
Columbia	Carolina Inn	883	799-8200	$42	$48
Columbia	Days Inn	883	736-0828	$23	$27
Columbia	Holiday Inn NW	883	794-9448	$32	$39
Columbia	Howard Johnsons	883	772-7288	$25	$27
Columbia	Quality Inn	883	772-8278	$34	$41
Columbia	Ramada Inn	883	796-2700	$36	$44
Columbia	Vagabond Inn	883	796-6240	$27	$38

(a)

```
Pennsylvania
Bedford Motel/Hotel: Crinoline Courts
   (814) 623-9511  S: $18  D: $28
Bedford Motel/Hotel: Holiday Inn
   (814) 623-9006  S: $29  D: $36
Bedford Motel/Hotel: Midway
   (814) 623-8107  S: $21  D: $26
Bedford Motel/Hotel: Penn Manor
   (814) 623-8177  S: $18  D: $25
Bedford Motel/Hotel: Quality Inn
   (814) 623-5188  S: $23  D: $28
Bedford Motel /Hotel: Terrace
   (814) 623-5111  S: $22  D: $24
Bradley Motel/Hotel: De Soto
   (814) 326-3567  S: $28  D: $24
Bradley Motel/Hotel: Holiday House
   (814) 362-4511  S: $22  D: $25
Bradley Motel/Hotel: Holiday Inn
   (814) 362-4581  S: $32  D: $40
Breezewood Motel/Hotel: Best Western Plaza
   (814) 735-4352  S: $28  D: $27
Breezewood Motel/Hotel: Motel 78
   (814) 735-4385  S: $16  D: $18
```

(b)

Figure 2.1   The structuring of text (Tullis, 1988)

Finding information in (b) invariably takes longer because it is cluttered. In (a) the information has been organized by grouping it into categories of hotel names, phone numbers and so on. The spacing between the columns also facilitates the perceptual processes in searching for an item.

Attention

Throughout our waking life our senses are constantly bombarded with sights, sounds, smells and so on. In order to make sense of this mass of information our cognitive processes limit the amount which we can attend to at any one time. This act of filtering is known as *selective attention*. The effect of this, however, is that our ability to perform more than one task at any time is limited.

The implications of our limited attention capabilities for system design are:

- How can people's attention be focused on the information that needs to be dealt with at any given stage of a task (for example, the display of critical error messages)?

- People are easily distracted. How is it possible to get their attention again without allowing them to miss any important information?

- How is it possible to allow people to switch between tasks at an interface (called multi-tasking)?

There are a number of techniques available to alert and direct users' attention. These include:

- the presentation of information in a logical and meaningful structure (see Section 4.3 for more detail) to help users to find relevant information

- the use of various visual markers (flashing lights, underlining, bold) and auditory cues (such as alarms) to get users' attention

- the partitioning of a screen into discrete or overlapping sections or windows (see Section 4.3) which can be readily associated with specific information, thus enabling users to carry out multiple tasks.

Human information processing

When interacting with a computer system a user will frequently look at a certain part of a screen and then perform an action (for example, scan a list of options on a menu and then select one). In cognitive psychology the way in which this is achieved has been regarded as a series of information processing stages. Sounds, sights and smells are all viewed in terms of information processing. The stages involved in human information processing are:

1 encoding the information from the environment into some form of internal · representation

2 comparing this representation with previously stored representations in the brain

3 deciding on an appropriate response

4 organizing a response and necessary action.

During the process of encoding, information is manipulated and restructured to provide us with a constant model of the world, as mentioned in the section on perception. The extent to which this information is then retained depends on how well it has been attended to and processed. Our ability to remember things, therefore, is closely linked to the way in which they are initially encoded.

Viewing the mind in terms of information processing has had many implications for HCI. In particular, it has provided the theoretical basis from which various design and evaluation tools (such as GOMS) have been developed (see Sections 3.3 and 6.3).

Memory

Memory is involved in all our actions. Talking, reading, writing and using a computer all need memory. Without memory we would not be able to perform the simplest of actions such as brushing our teeth, since we would not remember what to do with the brush. Our ability to remember things, however, is highly variable. This is particularly true with computer systems. Some operations are straightforward and take minimal effort to memorize while others take for ever to learn – and often drop out of memory soon after they have been used.

Example

Several systems use a large number of command names which are supposed to reflect the meaning of the underlying referent. In many cases, however, they can be quite obscure so that it is difficult to remember which operations they refer to.

For example, try working out the meaning of the names GREP and LINT which were designed for the Unix® operating system. (GREP allows the user to specify a string which is then searched for in a file and LINT checks a source code program in a file.) Names such as these often originate from strange links conjured up in the designer's mind which are clearly lost on the user. Icons also can suffer the same fate in that they may have initially meant something to the designer but become ambiguous when presented to users. See Figures 2.2 and 2.3 for examples.

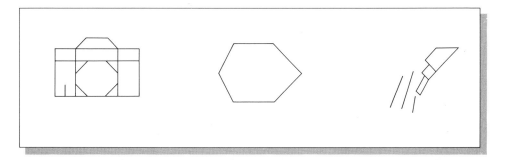

Figure 2.2   Examples of potentially ambiguous icons (Rogers, 1989)

Guidelines derived from cognitive psychology suggest various ways in which interfaces can be designed to make minimal demands on our memory. These include:

- using only names and icons that are meaningful and easily distinguishable from each other in a set (see Section 4.3 on screen design)
- using names and icons that reflect the structure of and the relationships between the various entities in the set (commands, menu options, and so on).

SAVE SORT FIND HELP PRINT
(a)

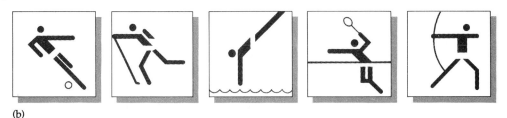

(b)

Figure 2.3   Examples of unambiguous command names (a) and icons (b). ((b) Mills, 1984)

(NB: The extent to which they are effective depends on other factors such as the size of the command set. See Section 4.3 for more details)

One of the most established findings in memory research is that *we can recognize material* from a display *far more easily than we can recall it* when not looking at the display.

Many user interfaces are now being designed to exploit this phenomenon. For example, menu-based systems (see Section 4.4) are now common. Rather than have to learn and then *recall* a set of obscure names or command abbreviations, users only have to *recognize* and select options and operations with which they are highly familiar.

Learning

Learning to use a computer is a complex process. Many designers have paid only scant attention to how people learn to use computer systems. New users are often viewed as passive beings who can absorb the contents of a manual and translate this information into a form that will allow them to use a system. It is important to realize that this is *not* the case. People who are only given a thick manual and told to 'get on with it' will often soon give up. Those who persevere frequently develop inefficient strategies and only ever use a fraction of the available functions.

Learning to use a computer requires *active involvement*. During this critical phase learners will call upon a number of different active learning strategies. These include:

- *Learning through doing*. People prefer to get on with doing something and seeing the outcome of their actions rather than wade through a manual.

- *Learning by active thinking*. Users need to understand how a system works and why it behaves in certain ways. They attempt this by generating their own explanations and *ad hoc* reasoning. If a system is not sufficiently *transparent* (that is, makes obvious the way actions should be performed, the way information is structured in the system, the meaning of icons, and so on) a user can develop an inaccurate understanding which in due course may result in incorrect operation. (See Mack *et al.* (1983) for extensive discussion of how people attempt to understand computer systems.)

- *Learning through goal and plan knowledge*. Users have some goal in mind which they must translate into a plan of action. To accomplish the goal their actions have to match the operations by which the computing system can achieve the desired end. In many cases there is a mismatch between the two, resulting in errors. (See Norman (1988) for a detailed description of this process.)

- *Learning through analogy*. Users compare an unfamiliar system with previously learned familiar concepts (for example, a word processor is *like* a typewriter). This is the most common form of learning. (See Carroll *et al.* (1988a) for an overview.)

- *Learning from errors*. Feedback from making a mistake can help people to learn and understand an activity. (See Lewis and Norman (1986) for a discussion.)

Learners also learn from information and cues they gather from the context or situation in which they work (Suchman, 1987).

To make the learning of computer systems easier, active methods of teaching which aid the above processes should be explored. Various techniques that have been developed include:

- *The minimal manual*. The content of a manual is greatly reduced and the manual is made task oriented. (See Carroll *et al.*, 1988b.)

- *The training wheels scenario*. The functionality of a system is at first limited to simple operations to protect the learner from carrying out any actions that could have drastic and undesirable consequences. (See Carroll and Ray, 1988.)

- *Metaphors*. A concrete model with which the user is familiar is provided at an interface. This enables users to exploit their existing knowledge of other domains when learning to use a system. The most well-known example is the desktop metaphor.

Models

When we interact with anything, be it the environment, other people or technological artefacts, we form internal *mental models* of ourselves interacting with them. When 'run' or 'rehearsed', these mental models provide the basis from which we can predict and explain our interactions (Norman and Draper, 1986).

Example

A simple example of *running* a mental model is trying to think of the number of windows or rooms in your house. To perform this operation most people have to count the number of windows or rooms mentally by imagining walking through the house or around it. In terms of computing systems, mental models enable us to understand the workings of a system and to make predictions about the outcome of various actions.

A *user's mental model* of a system is built up from prior experience, interactions with a user interface, its behaviour and documentation. Collectively, the parts of the system are called the *system image* (Norman and Draper, 1986). The design team have a *design model* (sometimes referred to as a *conceptual model*) of the way they think the system should work. (See Figure 2.4.) The design model is explicit and concrete, and seeks to be a complete and consistent model of a system. A user, however, will normally only ever develop a partial mental model of a system, which in many cases will be changeable, simplified and subject to distortion. When designing a system image, therefore, it is important to make aspects of the design model *transparent*, *coherent* and *supportive*.

People who work together and use the same system (e.g. a network) have a *distributed model*. Each user in a group has a different, but overlapping, model of the same system. The extent to which the models are distributed varies with the type of interaction and activity. Research in this area is important for the development of successful collaborative systems (Sections 2.3 and 4.6). Mental models or design models are not to be confused with *user models*. These are cognitive and performance models of the user which have been developed by researchers to provide design and evaluative tools (see Chapters 3 and 6).

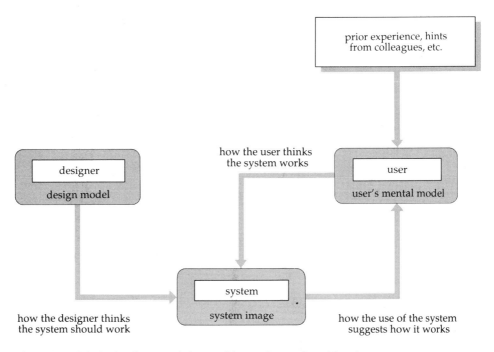

Figure 2.4   Distinction between design model, users' mental model and system image

The use of metaphor at a user interface

It is important to design a system image that enables a user to develop a suitable mental model. A technique that was mentioned earlier is to design an explicit metaphor that is appropriate for the system. The problem, however, is deciding which metaphor will best match a task. The key factor is ensuring that the actions, procedures and concepts of the familiar domain map as closely as possible on to the application structures that are to be represented at the user interface. In addition, it is important that the user understands the limitations of the metaphor.

Example

As part of the desktop metaphor it is common practice to include an icon of a wastebasket on the 'desk'. Not only does this contravene our expectations as to where to find wastebaskets (on the floor), but also the interface wastebasket has other functions apart from its conventional use as a container for discarded objects. For instance, the wastebasket is often the place where disk icons are put in order to eject the corresponding disk from the disk drive. This implies that one has to 'throw away' a disk in order to retrieve it! Such an apparent contradiction can cause conceptual problems to first-time users since it is easy to think that the contents of the disk will be discarded when the disk is placed in the wastebasket.

Drawing by Koren; © 1979 The New Yorker Magazine, Inc.

Table 2.1 shows examples of interface metaphors (that is, metaphors explicitly represented at an interface) which have been developed for various applications.

Table 2.1   Examples of applications and associated metaphors

Application area	Metaphor	Similar to
Operating environment	The desktop	Office tasks, file management
Spreadsheets	Ledger sheet	Numerical tables
Object-oriented environments	Physical world	Real-world behaviour
Hypertext	Notecards	Flexible organization of structured text
Multi-media environments	Rooms (each associated with a different medium/task)	Spatial structure of buildings
Computer-supported co-operative work	Agents	Cultural knowledge

Note that the term *metaphor* can also refer to the analogic reasoning that a user may perform even when there is no concrete model at an interface. An example is a word processor which is *like* a typewriter.

2.3   *Organizational and social aspects*

So far in this section we have focused primarily upon the psychology of a single user interacting with a single computer system. This has been a dominant perspective for HCI for the last ten years but it is not the only one: organizational and social psychology are important too. Most work – and for that matter play or any social interaction – involves groups of people interacting with each other, with various natural and manufactured objects, and with the environment in which they are placed.

The social aspects of computer-supported co-operative working (CSCW) are now an important research topic and there are many projects which are examining the way people use electronic mail, electronic conferencing and other forms of collaborative system. If such systems are to be successful researchers and developers need to understand such issues as:

- what kinds of tasks people wish to do

- what they want the technology to do for them

- how they communicate with each other and whether the technology facilitates or hinders this communication

- what their working and organizational environments are like and so on (see Section 4.6 for a brief discussion of CSCW).

However, these issues are not new. As Eason (1988) and Bjorn-Anderson (1986) have pointed out, they need to be considered in relation to any organization that introduces new technology if the benefits shown in Figure 2.5 are to be gained. Ignoring the effects of new technology can result in:

- unhappy staff

- high staff turnover

- reduced productivity.

Figure 2.5   Information technology benefits in the office (Eason, 1988)

In a study described by Eason (1988), that was carried out in North America, only twenty per cent of the systems introduced into organizations achieved their intended benefits (Figure 2.6).

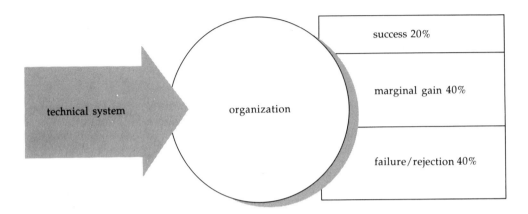

Figure 2.6   Success rates in information technology (Eason, 1988)

In a competitive world cost is a significant factor. Whilst hardware costs are decreasing significantly the organizational costs of implementing new technology can be very high (Figure 2.7), so it is essential that significant benefits result from the investment.

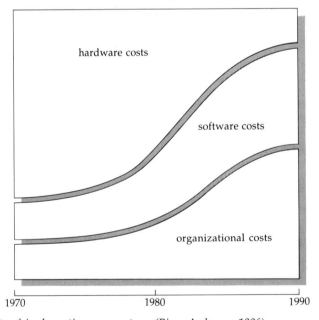

Figure 2.7   Costs of implementing new systems (Bjørn-Andersen, 1986)

Organizational and social change

The introduction of new technology inevitably leads to changes in the structure of jobs and the organization itself, which can be problematic.

> Frequently these matters are dealt with in an *ad hoc* way as problems arise and constitute a piecemeal and unsystematic way of changing from one form of organisation to another. It is a strange counterpoint to the planning of the technical systems which is often highly structured and rational.
> (Eason, 1988, p. 107)

The type of management to which Eason refers often leads to frustration and under-utilization of the new system. However, technology itself does not improve or degrade peoples' jobs: it is the way it is used that matters. Figure 2.8 shows how technology can have either a positive or negative effect. Depending upon whether the technology becomes a tool or simply exerts control, it can:

- change the nature of jobs

- change the way people feel

- increase productivity

- have an enormous impact on the organization.

'... and to think I bought this system to replace six bookkeepers.'
Datamation, September 1982

Some of the working practices that may change as a result of introducing new technology include:

- *Job content.* Who does what, when, and how much (computers often make things more formal rather than less formal).

- *Personnel policies.* Probably as a result of changes to job content (e.g. confidentiality of information).

- *Job satisfaction.* Motivation, control, financial and other rewards, learning new skills.

- *Power and influence.* This may shift between individuals or groups.

- *Working environment.* Changes in space and equipment allocation.

An example of a positive outcome is job enrichment through more variation and learning new skills.

Example

An example might be a clerical worker who does word processing and telephone follow-up for a group of customers, instead of performing only one task for a much larger group of customers.

An example of a negative outcome is that the job becomes more routine and the volume of work increases, creating bottle-necks.

Example

Eason (1988) found that doctors were able to make laboratory test requests in batches after the introduction of a new system which was much easier and quicker than the old procedure. The result was that the laboratory was over-run with test requests. The laboratory had not been provided with any additional resources to cope with this unpredicted extra load and hence could not maintain the service doctors relied on.

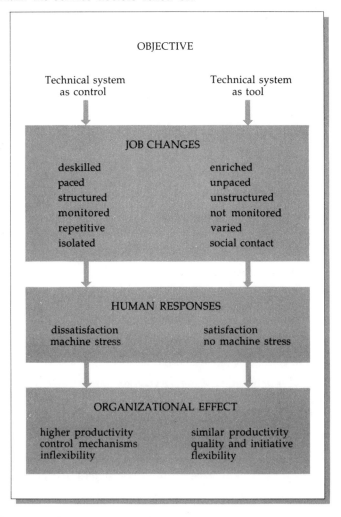

Figure 2.8 The impact of information technology on jobs (Eason, 1988)

2.4 How to apply psychology

It is one thing to consider the important issues surrounding the human element but it is another to apply this knowledge effectively in order to design better information technology. Having access to the research findings and theories of psychology is only a *first step* in that it provides a framework in which to view a design problem. The *second step* requires developing a means by which this information can be *translated into a usable form* by designers, managers and programmers.

Experts in HCI have been developing methods and tools specifically for this purpose. Essentially, three approaches have evolved. These are:

- *Prescriptive approaches*. Principles derived from psychological findings and theory are extracted and translated into 'packaged' guidelines and standards (see Section 3.6). This is the most widely used approach.

- *Predictive approaches*. Theories based on the notion of human information processing are transformed into user models which are then used to predict how users will perform with different interfaces (see Chapter 6). Much research is being pursued in this area.

- *Empirical approaches*. Concepts, methods and frameworks taken from psychology are applied to an interface design problem. This is common among researchers but costly and time-consuming (see Chapter 3).

Whether designing new technology, implementing it within an organization or evaluating its effectiveness, it is advisable to contact HCI experts and human factors consultants in the first instance. It may also be possible to have an in-house HCI specialist group who work closely with other members of a design team and act as the critical link between the team and the end-users.

Developing a computer system is a complex activity. It involves determining what the system will do (the functionality) and how it will do it (the operational aspects). In terms of the user interface, this means designing the way that users communicate with the system.

'Someday all these people will have personal computers, and it will be a much, much better world.'

3.1 System development life-cycle

Computer software development normally follows a number of stages, as shown in Figure 3.1, starting with project selection and ending with a maintainable implemented system. User involvement in this cycle may be very limited.

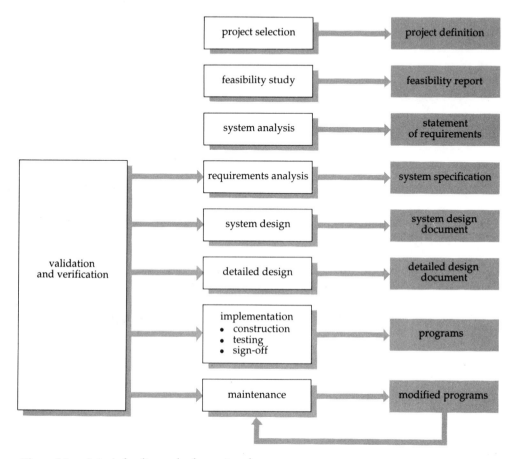

Figure 3.1 A typical software development cycle

Some factors that influence the degree of user involvement include:

- the design team's knowledge of HCI
- the type of system being developed:
  - *generic systems* are sold on the open market with no specific organization in mind; there is often little involvement with users during the design process
  - *bespoke systems* are commissioned by an organization for its own use, so there tends to be close involvement with the user organization although not necessarily with end-users
- incompatibility of HCI methods with software engineering methods.

3.2   Modern approaches to system development

A number of ways have been proposed to incorporate users' opinions and needs into system development.

Structured methods

A major development in software design has been the introduction of structured design methods such as the Jackson structured design methodology (JSD) (Jackson, 1975) and structured systems analysis and design methodology (SSADM) (Downes, Clare and Coe, 1991). Such methods promote a disciplined way of working.

Structured design methods also formalize the relationship between users and developers as an explicit client–contractor arrangement and thus attempt to increase user involvement. However, there may still be little direct contact with end-users.

Participative methods

Participative methods take social and organizational requirements into account at an early stage in the development cycle. Users participate in analysing organizational requirements and in planning appropriate social and technical structures to support both individual and organizational needs.

One of the best known of the participative methodologies is the 'effective technical and human implementation of computer systems' method (better known as ETHICS) developed by Mumford (1983). This analysis explores organizational issues, for example goals, values and sources of job satisfaction, as well as traditional information flows and key tasks.

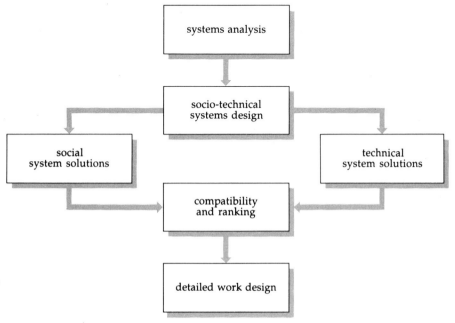

Figure 3.2   The ETHICS method (Eason, 1988)

When technical and social constraints have been identified, design options are prescribed in terms of people, organization and computerized support. Specific recommendations about the behaviour and appearance of the computer interface are not made.

User-centred design

A key aim of HCI is to make users the focus of design activity, hence the term 'user-centred design'. This is achieved by involving users and taking their needs into account throughout the design process.

Principles

Some principles for involving users in design are:

• Focus on the users and the users' needs, and in so doing make user issues rather than technical considerations central in the design process.

• Carry out a task analysis in which details of the users' tasks and information about the task environment are collected, so that users' needs are well understood. Task analysis needs to be done in addition to a general requirements analysis, which tends to focus on *what* functionality is required and not on *how* to provide that functionality (see Section 3.3).

• Carry out early testing and evaluation with users to ensure that the system is designed to meet their needs (see Chapter 6).

• Design iteratively with many cycles of 'design – test with users – redesign'. Do not expect to produce one 'right' solution which is not changed, but instead aim to design an evolving system which is tailored to users' needs more with each iteration.

General practices

The development cycle in user-centred design is similar to the one in Figure 3.3.

Early design is dominated by collecting and synthesizing information about users' needs and capabilities. The main techniques for obtaining this information are task analysis, requirements analysis (Section 3.3) and usability tests (Section 3.3 and Chapter 6). Using this information the design team develop a conceptual model of the system (Section 2.2). Part of this conceptual design involves deciding what the dialogue between the user and the system will be like (Section 4.4) which, in turn, determines the system image (Section 2.2).

The conceptual design of an interface generally involves creating sketches of screens which demonstrate surface features of the system (the representational aspects). These sketches can then be tested with users to establish their appropriateness. For example, a design team may need to check that the metaphor (Section 2.2) on which they have based their design is useful to users.

As the design develops it will be transformed through various forms of specification (Sections 3.3 and 3.4) and prototypes (Section 5.4) through to

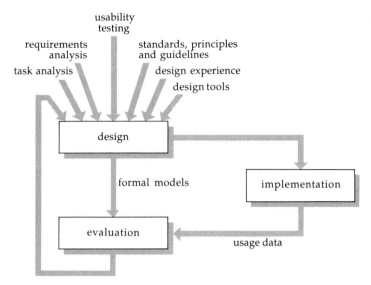

*Figure 3.3
A typical user-centred design cycle (adapted from Perlman, 1988)*

implementation. Design principles, standards and guidelines (Section 3.6) will guide the process and it will be supported by computer-based prototyping techniques (Section 5.4) and design tools (Section 5.2).

3.3   Early design stages

In any kind of product development it is essential to find out what users want the product to do, how they will use it, what kind of design will be liked and how much people will pay for it.

'Your carburettor's way off. Your valves are so-so. Your VISA balance is just fine.'

Market research provides information about general market requirements, while three types of technique are used to obtain information about specific design requirements:

- *Requirements analysis* specifies *what* the system should do (that is, the system's *functionality*).
- *Task analysis* provides information about *how* it should be done.
- *Usability testing* defines the *acceptable performance* of the system for specific types of user carrying out specific tasks.

Traditionally, requirements analysis has been carried out as a routine part of system design by software engineers, whereas task analysis and usability testing have evolved from HCI practice as a means of developing user-centred systems.

Requirements analysis

Systems analysts obtain information about users' requirements by using techniques such as interviews and questionnaires and by observing and analysing current practice. From an initial statement of the customers' requirements software engineers produce a *system specification.*

The problem with traditional requirements analysis is that detailed information about what the real users actually do and how they do it is often not collected. Consequently, designers often fulfil the requirements specified by management without taking account of the real needs of users.

'The trouble is, it's been programmed to cut a longer lawn.'

Task analysis

In an attempt to make the process of collecting and abstracting information about users' tasks easier and more systematic, HCI specialists have developed a number of task analysis methods. These range from the 'macro' methods, in which the whole system is analysed in terms of organizational, social, and environmental aspects, to 'micro' methods in which discrete tasks are decomposed into hierarchical structures and finally into small cognitive units.

Examples of 'macro' techniques

- *ETHICS* (already mentioned in Section 3.2) focuses on the context of tasks and its influence on the way that users perform their tasks (Mumford, 1983).

- *Open system task analysis (OSTA)* follows a socio-technical systems analysis model in which technical requirements (that is, functionality) are specified alongside social system requirements (that is, usability and acceptability). Its underlying aim is to provide a methodology for understanding the transformation that occurs when a computer system is introduced into a working environment (Eason and Harker, 1980).

- User System Task Match (USTM) (MacCaulay *et al.*, 1990) is an attempt to tackle the problems of requirements specification. It recognizes the importance of coupling structured methods with additional human factors input and employs tree-like diagrammatic task models and English for specifying system requirements.

Flowcharts and natural language descriptions are the main ways of describing the information collected with these methods.

Examples of 'intermediate' techniques

- *Generic hierarchical task analysis (HTA)* and the many hybrid forms of HTA are used by most industrial analysts. The aim of HTA is to describe the task in terms of a hierarchical tree of subtasks. A point numbering notation is used for describing plans.

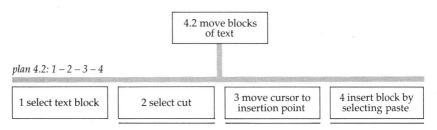

Figure 3.4   An HTA extract for moving blocks of text in Microsoft® Word

Variations of HTA include its adaptation to deal with:

- hierarchical planning (Sebillotte, 1988) where the emphasis is on users' goals rather than on the operations that users carry out at a computer interface.

- techniques for charting the events and necessary responses in air traffic control (Philips *et al.*, 1988).

Examples of 'micro' techniques

Micro-level analysis techniques are concerned with cognitive modelling, in which the aim is to model the cognitive knowledge and physical actions that users must carry out in order to do a task. Typically these techniques involve a hierarchical decomposition of a small task such as editing a line from a document. These are very fine grain analysis techniques, which are also used in analytic evaluation (see Section 6.3).

- The *GOMS* family of models (Card *et al.* 1983) consists of descriptions of the *methods* needed to accomplish specified *goals*. (The acronym stands for 'goals, operators, methods and selection rules'.) The methods are a series of steps consisting of operations (that is, *operators*) that a user performs. When there is more than one method available to accomplish a goal the GOMS model has *selection rules* to choose the appropriate method.

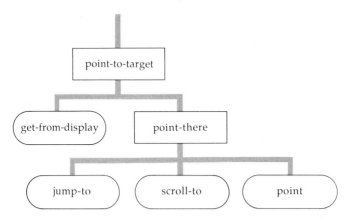

Figure 3.5   An excerpt from the GOMS model for the Bravo word processor (Card et al., 1983)

There are three basic levels of granularity in the models used in a GOMS analysis:

- The *GOMS model* describes the *general* methods for accomplishing a *set* of tasks.
- The *unit task level* breaks users' tasks into subtasks, called *unit tasks*, and then estimates the time that it takes for the user to perform these.
- The *keystroke-level model* describes and predicts the time it takes to perform a task by specifying the keystrokes needed.

Depending on which of these forms of model is used, the analysis may be specified hierarchically or as a flat representation. The original GOMS specification was cumbersome and has been replaced by a more natural specification language called 'natural GOMS language' or NGOMS (Kieras, 1988).

- *Cognitive complexity theory (CCT)* (Kieras and Polson, 1985) has been developed from the basic GOMS model and has the same basic aims. Using this technique, users' *how-to-do-it* knowledge of a system (the users' task representation) is partitioned from their knowledge of *how a system works* (the users' device representation) and the *overall context* in which tasks are performed (the job–task environment). This technique can be automated and the specification used as the basis for an executable prototype (see Sections 3.4 and 5.4).

- *Command language grammar (CLG)* was developed by Moran (1981). It is a top-down approach consisting of four main levels and, as the name suggests, it is based upon a grammar. Each level is itself a *complete description* of the system from the perspective of that level and connects with the levels above and below it. The levels provide a valuable way of viewing the interface but using the notation is not simple.

- *Task–action grammar (TAG)* (Payne and Green, 1986) has been developed to model the relationships between users' tasks and actions. It uses a formal specification language similar to BNF (see Section 3.4) as 'a grammar of the head'. The actions in a given task are described in terms of keystrokes, mouse movements and other actions. Reisner (1981) also adapted BNF to map users' interactions at the interfaces of two systems in an evaluation study (see Section 3.4 and Chapter 6).

- *Task analysis for knowledge-based descriptions (TAKD)* (Johnson *et al.*, 1985; Diaper, 1989) is a task analysis method in which tasks are described in terms of the knowledge necessary to do them. This technique has been used to analyse IT training material as well as tasks done with computer systems.

Usability testing

Whereas the results of a task analysis are generally geared towards the specification of a new system, usability testing is primarily intended to provide information for the upgrading and maintenance of existing systems. In this sense it encompasses evaluation. (See Section 6.3 for details of techniques.)

When usability testing is integrated into the design cycle by being quantitatively specified in advance, it is known as *usability engineering* because of similarities with engineering practices.

The key aspects of interest (Shackel, 1990) in usability testing are:

- *learnability* – the time and effort required to reach a specified level of user performance (also described as 'ease of learning')

- *throughput* – the tasks accomplished by experienced users, the speed of task execution and the errors made (also described as 'ease of use')

- *flexibility* – the extent to which users can adapt a system to new ways of interaction as they become more experienced

- *attitude* – the positive attitude engendered in users by the system.

The majority of usability studies focus on user performance in terms of learnability, throughput and users' attitudes because they are the easiest characteristics to measure.

The measures that are collected for describing usability are referred to as *usability metrics*. Examples of metrics used to assess learnability include completion time for a specified task by a specified set of users, the number of errors per task and the time spent on using documentation.

Metrics are fed into the design cycle using a *usability specification* together with functional requirements.

Example

The attribute of concern is the 'installability' of a system, and the measure used to evaluate the system is the amount of time taken to carry out an installation. The metrics specified in Table 3.1 are for 'worst case', 'planned level' and 'best case'.

Table 3.1 A sample row from a usability specification

Attribute	Measuring method	Worst case	Planned level	Best case	Present level
Installability	Time to install	1 day with media	1 hour without media	10 minutes with media	Many can't install

(Whiteside *et al.*, 1988, p. 801)

Impact analysis (Whiteside *et al.*, 1988) provides a way of ranking users' problems in order of their importance to the total usability of a system.

The common objective underlying usability testing and task analysis is to assess how usable a system is going to be.

3.4   Later design stages

Regardless of the methods or techniques used in a design, it is important that the results are in a form that can be communicated between designers and users.

At the beginning of a design project a statement of requirements (which includes details from the task analysis and usability tests) must be developed. Designers need to understand what kind of system their clients need and clients need to understand what is technically feasible. One straightforward and non-technical communication medium is preferable, although several may be combined:

- natural language description
- diagrams
- some form of non-executable prototype, such as a series of screen mock-ups, which may even be filmed and presented as a video.

The aim is to make key aspects of the future system visible to clients so that they may provide feedback for the designers. Later on in the design process a more precise form of specification is usually needed for communication of technical detail among members of the design team.

The main trade-off between formal and informal notations is the degree of precision possible versus the time and skill required to produce such precision.

- *Formal* notations are rigorous and on the whole unambiguous, but they are very time-consuming to use and often require considerable expertise both to use and understand.

- *Informal* kinds of notation are relatively easy to use and can be understood without any specialist training but they are too vague for detailed technical design work.

Formal specification methods are being developed for HCI but they are very new and as yet have not been applied to large-scale system development.

One way in which HCI researchers have tried to overcome the problem of specification is by adapting software engineering methods. Two examples are:

- *Backus–Naur form* – a grammatical notation
- *transition diagrams* – graphic structures indicating states and transitions from one state to another.

Backus–Naur form (BNF)

BNF is a formal grammar that has been used to describe programming languages. The notation takes the form of rules for producing correct statements – *production rules*. The advantage is that BNF can be programmed, thus allowing the completeness and consistency of a design to be checked automatically. The main disadvantage is that BNF is difficult to read and write.

Example

In the following example the vertical lines mean OR and the symbol ::= means 'is made up of' or 'contains'. For instance, the first line in the BNF description that follows means that a command can be either the CREATE, DELETE or STOP command. The subsequent lines define each of these commands in turn so that the precise nature of each one has been defined.

```
<command> ::= <create_command> | <delete_command> |
              <stop_command>

<create_command> ::= CREATE <item_type> <item_name>
                     AT <value><value>
        :
        :
<item_type> ::= TRIANGLE | SQUARE

<item_name> ::= 1 to 6 alphabetic characters

<value> ::= integer
```

An example of the way that BNF can be applied to HCI is provided by Reisner (1981) who used it to describe user actions at an interface. One of the main reasons for doing this was to define formally the difference in usability between two systems using an 'action language' based on BNF. TAG (described in Section 3.3) also uses a notation based on BNF.

Transition diagrams

Transition diagrams (also called *finite state* and *state transition diagrams*) show the availability of functions at any point in an interface dialogue. They provide:

- a syntactic description of all *states* that are apparent to a user
- the available courses of *action* from those states
- the *transitions* between states.

As Figure 3.6 shows, a transition diagram is composed of three basic elements: *states* (called *nodes* and represented by circles), *transitions* (called *arcs* and represented by arrows) and *action* or *response* labels.

A state is a stable condition in which a system awaits some event such as user input; it is identified by a label inside a circle. A transition is the process of progressing from one state to another, or to the same state; it is initiated by the occurrence of an event such as an action by the user. Arrows show the direction of the flow of control from one state to another. Each transition is labelled with an action name which is usually paired with a response name. Actions define the conditions under which transitions occur.

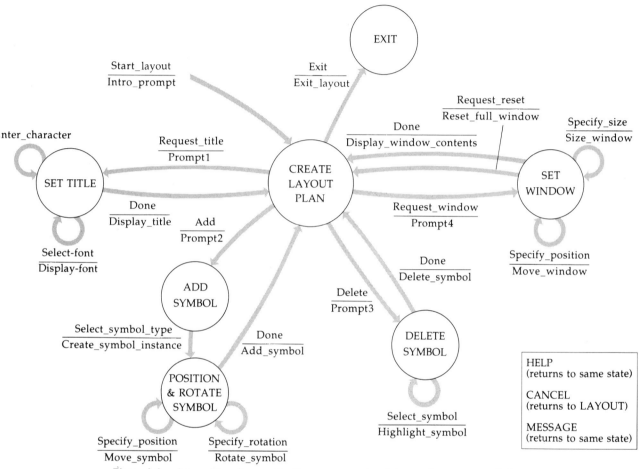

Figure 3.6 A transition diagram for the user–computer dialogue of a program called LAYOUT (Foley et al., 1982)

The major problem with using transition diagrams to describe a user interface is that they quickly become large and complicated.

A general difficulty with this and any formalism is that it is difficult to visualize the appearance of a system and how it will work.

Wasserman and Shewmake (1985) have attempted to overcome these problems by adapting the formalism so that it is executable and they have developed a prototyping system based on executable transition diagrams (see Section 5.4 on prototyping tools).

3.5   The relationships between methods

The relationship of some HCI methods and structured methods to the stages of the software development life cycle is shown in Figure 3.7. This analysis shows that:

- *Organizational methods* are concerned largely with the specification of the early stages of design.

- *Cognitive methods* are also concerned with early stages of design but are generally used later than organizational methods.

- *Software engineering methods* are primarily concerned with functional processes and data structures, usually taking no account of either cognitive aspects of the interface or organizational concerns.

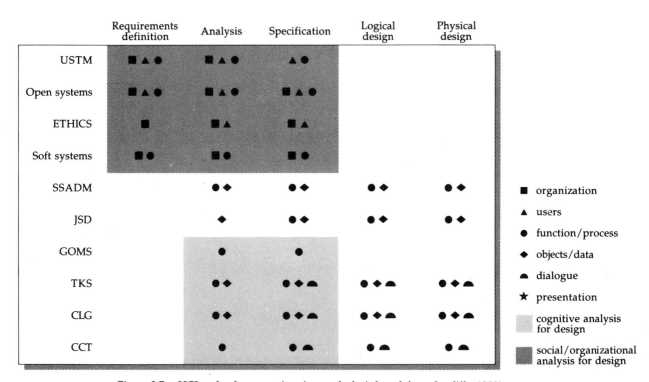

Figure 3.7   HCI and software engineering methods (adapted from Sutcliffe, 1989)

However, work is being carried out to explore ways of integrating HCI techniques and knowledge with structured software development methods such as JSD (Jackson, 1975) and SSADM (Downes *et al.*, 1991). (See also Section 3.2.)

3.6 Guidelines and standards

In order to develop and integrate a design, an interface designer needs to call on a number of sources of information:

- *scientific knowledge*, such as cognitive psychology (Section 2.2) and organizational psychology (Section 2.3)

- *established techniques* for input, output and user support provision such as menus and forms (Section 4.4), cursor control (Section 4.1) and online aids (Section 4.5)

- *experience* of other designs and knowledge of other systems (Section 4.6).

Knowledge, techniques and experience do not, however, *apply* themselves to a specific problem.

Guidelines occur in several forms:

- High-level and universally applicable design *principles* need to be employed to direct the design and integrate ideas on design into a sound framework.

- *Design rules* are sometimes used to instruct a designer how to achieve a principled design that is appropriate for the particular system in question.

- Systems should conform to international, national and industry *standards*.

Ultimately, there are only good and bad design decisions, which reflect the way in which design guidelines are applied. Designers need to choose and apply the right guidelines intelligently at the right time. Attitude, experience, insight and common sense help in this process.

Guidelines

The term *guidelines* encompasses both the broad principles, which offer general advice and provide a sound foundation for a design, and the specific design rules, which direct details of a design. Guidelines are found in a variety of places:

- Professional, trade and academic journal articles provide a good source of information about current practice and experience.

- General handbooks offer a coherent and comprehensive coverage of the area. Two particularly good books are Smith and Mosier's *Guidelines for Designing User Interface Software* (1986) and Gaines and Shaw's highly readable book *The Art of Computer Conversation* (1984), which describes guidelines in terms of general 'proverbs'.

- House style guides detail the standard functional and display techniques for particular computers or organizations. For example, Apple Computer's *Inside Macintosh* describes the use of the Macintosh style windows, scroll bars and icons.

In a brief introduction such as this, we cannot hope to cover all the details of guidelines; however, in most reviews, a number of principles stand out.

- *Know the user population.* This can be difficult to achieve, especially when a diverse population of users has to be accommodated or when the user population can only be anticipated in the most general terms. Knowing the user includes being sympathetic to different user needs by, for example, providing program short-cuts for knowledgeable users, promoting the 'personal worth' of the individual user and allowing users to perform tasks in more than one way.

- *Reduce cognitive load.* This concerns designing so that users do not have to remember large amounts of detail (Section 2.2). Methods for achieving this include:
  - *Minimize memorization* by using techniques such as selecting from a menu rather than remembering command names, using names for objects rather than numbers, and giving the user access to (understandable) system documentation. However, care must be taken to apply principles appropriately.

  Example

  The famous short-term memory limitation (Miller, 1956, that people can remember only 7 ± 2 things) does not mean that menus should be restricted to seven options! Users need not remember specific items in any detail if they can select from a displayed list.

  - *Minimize learning* by being consistent, drawing on knowledge of similar systems and by choosing meaningful names and symbols.

- *Engineer for errors.* A common excuse is that a problem occurred because of 'human error'. But people will always make errors and indeed *have* to make errors in order to learn. Engineering for errors includes taking forcing actions which prevent the user from making an error (or at least make it more difficult!), providing good error messages, using reversible actions which allow users to correct their own errors and providing a large number of explicit diagnostics. (See Section 2.2.)

- *Maintain consistency and clarity.* Consistency emerges from standard operations and representations and from using appropriate metaphors (Section 2.2) that help to build and maintain a user's mental model of a system. A designer can only have ideas about what is clear based on initial information about users. Designs *must* be confirmed with users – through prototyping (Section 5.4) and evaluating designs (Chapter 6) – to be certain that the system's interface really is clear.

Guidelines inevitably contain some overlapping and contradictory advice. Consistency might, for example, be important for learning to use a particular system but troublesome when a user becomes experienced. Many of these contradictions appear early and then disappear during the design process. Often the constraints imposed by the characteristics of the users, the tasks and the environment will remove the need to choose between contradictory items of advice, because one guideline will clearly apply when others do not.

Standards

Standards concern prescribed ways of discussing, presenting or doing something. Standards seek to achieve some form of *consistency* across products which are of the same type. We are familiar with standards in many walks of life – standard colours for electrical wiring, standard controls on cars, standard shoe and clothing sizes. Establishing standards encourages:

- *A common terminology*. For example, standard measures of usability (*usability metrics*, Section 3.3) or performance mean that designers and users know that they are discussing the same concept. All systems of the same type can be subjected to a standard benchmark that facilitates comparisons.

- *Maintainability and evolvability*. Standard implementation techniques facilitate program maintenance because all programs can be expected to have a shared style and structure. Additional facilities can be added to a system if its external interfaces are of a standard form.

- *A common identity*. An in-house or industry standard for display style or screen layout ensures that all systems have the same 'look and feel' and are easily recognizable.

- *Reduction in training*. Knowledge can be more easily transferred from one system to another if standard command keys and other interaction techniques are adopted.

- *Health and safety*. Users are less likely to be surprised by unexpected system behaviour if standard controls and warnings are used. Health is promoted by attendance to standard working practices.

Standards are developed and promoted by a number of different organizations for a number of different reasons:

- *Governments*. Examples are the European Community directives on safety and health in the workplace (Directive 89/391/EEC) and for display screens (Directive 90/270/EEC).

- *National and international organizations*. The portable common tools environment (PCTE, Section 5.3) is a standard program interface promoted by the European Community through its Esprit initiative (*PCTE Functional Specification*, 1986). All systems developed under this programme are encouraged to conform to this standard. The International Standards Organization (ISO) is the main international organization concerned with standards. It works closely with the American National Standards Institute (ANSI) and the British Standards Institution (BSI).

- *Professional bodies* such as the British Computer Society (BCS), the Institute of Electrical Engineers (IEE) and the Institute of Electrical and Electronic Engineers (IEEE) also develop and promote standards.

- *Industry standards* help with transferring knowledge from one system to another and in providing a common identity. For example, the software development company Microsoft uses standard command keys on all its products.

- *De facto standards* exist. For example, the QWERTY keyboard is the standard English-language keyboard layout, but it evolved because of the mechanical limitations of early typewriters. Once a *de facto* standard has evolved and been widely adopted, it is usually too late to change it easily. Industry standards often become *de facto* standards which may subsequently become national or international standards.

- *House standards* are important, particularly in large organizations where commonality can be vital. House standards apply to diagram notation, documentation style, programming methods and so on.

Although there are still few standards in HCI, the subject is currently at the centre of much debate. The ISO, through Technical Committee TC159, Signals and Controls Group 4, Working Group 5 (TC159/SC4/WG5) is developing standards for principles of dialogue design, usability characteristics, usability assurance and design guidelines for specific types of dialogue and user assistance. For further information see Stewart, 1991.

Example

The Graphical Kernel Standard (GKS) was the first ISO graphics standard (ISO 7942; ISO, 1985). Another ISO group is looking at Open Systems Interconnection (OSI). In industry, X-windows (Scheifler *et al.*, 1988) is becoming the industry standard for windowing systems on workstations, and Unix® may become the industry standard operating system. There is now also an 'open' standard operating system that is a Unix® look-alike called Posix.

All organizations that develop systems should have a set of design standards and a copy of a good reference book on the shelf. When evaluating hardware and software systems, conformity with standards and guidelines should figure high on the selection criteria.

4.1 Input
Keyboards
Special keys and other facilities
Automatic scanners
Other input devices
Speech
Eye and head movement
4.2 Output
Visual output
Non-visual output
4.3 Screen design
Amount of information presented
Grouping of information
Highlighting of information
Standardization of screen display
Presentation of text
Graphics
The screen design process
4.4 Communication styles
Command languages
Menus
Natural language dialogue
Question and answer dialogues
Form-filling
Direct manipulation
4.5 User support
Online-based support
Document-based support
Instructor-based and expert-based support
4.6 Types of system

A designer of interactive computer systems faces a huge range of options. These options cover all aspects of an interface from the methods of input used, the style of the output and screen displays, to the overall 'look and feel' of the interaction and the user support available. This chapter examines the options available and illustrates some different types of system and their characteristics.

4.1 Input

Input is concerned with recording and entering data into the computer system and issuing instructions to the computer (commands). An *input device* is a device that, together with appropriate software, transforms data from the user into a form that the computer system can process. There is a vast array of different input devices.

Selecting an appropriate input device can be vital to the success of a system. The most appropriate input device will be the one that:

- matches the physiological and psychological characteristics of users, their training and their expertise. For example, older adults may be hampered by conditions such as arthritis and may be unable to type; inexperienced users may be unfamiliar with keyboard layout

- is appropriate for the tasks that are to be performed. For example, a drawing task requires an input device that allows continuous movement; selecting an option from a list requires an input device that permits discrete movement

- is suitable for its environment. For example, speech input is useful where there is no surface on which to put a keyboard; automatic scanning is suitable if there is a large amount of data to be gathered.

Keyboards

The most common input device is the keyboard or keypad. Although most are based on the familiar typewriter keyboard, there are a number of other more specialized keyboards. Table 4.1 lists some different keyboards.

Table 4.1 Types of keyboard

Device	Description	Key features
QWERTY keyboard (The continental European equivalent is called AZERTY)	Uses the most common arrangement of alphabetic keys.	Required when the data to be input are highly variable. Many people are trained for using it. Very slow for those not trained.
Dvorak keyboard	Similiar to the QWERTY keyboard, but keys allow for more efficient input.	People familiar with the QWERTY keyboard need retraining.
Alphabetic keyboard	Similar to the QWERTY but with the arrangement in alphabetical order.	Often thought to be suitable for people untrained in keyboard use, but tests show that it is no faster for an untrained user to locate a letter than either of the two previous keyboards.
Chord keyboard	Various arrangements. To form words (usually in a short-hand type notation), several keys are pressed simultan-eously.	Can be extremely fast when used by a trained operator. Used to record transcripts of court proceedings, Parliament, etc. Requires training to use and to read the output. The right type can be suitable for the visually impaired when coupled with a Braille or speech output device.
Numeric keypad	Number keys, arithmetic operator keys (plus, minus, multiply, divide), decimal point and enter key.	Good for very fast keying of numeric data. Trained operators can reach a very high speed. Untrained users find it easy to use.

Figure 4.1   Simplified Dvorak keyboard (Norman, 1988)

Special keys and other facilities

Most input devices have some form of an 'enter' function key (often written
<enter>) which indicates when the input should be sent to the computer. In
addition, many input devices have a number of special-purpose or *function keys*,
which, rather than simply entering data, perform a particular *action*. Some
systems provide similar facilities through the use of *buttons* and *bars* on the
screen. Table 4.2 lists some common methods of performing specific actions or
commands.

Table 4.2 Special keys and facilities

Device	Description	Key features
Cursor control keys	Four keys with arrows showing the direction in which a cursor on the screen will move when the key is pressed.	Used for moving around a screen display. Most appropriate for text displays as the keys usually move the cursor one character or line at a time.
'Soft' function keys or control keys	Keys that are pressed in combination with another key (usually called the 'control' key, written <ctrl>) to cause some action to take place.	Keys are programmed to perform the action. Can be used in place of cursor keys (e.g. <ctrl> and D pressed together move the cursor down one line of the display). Good for commonly used functions and for providing quick execution of commands. Can be difficult to remember. No standard arrangement.
'Hard' function keys	Labelled keys which perform a function (e.g. <PgDn> will move the display down one screen length).	Cursor keys and the <enter> key are examples. Less obscure than soft function keys since they are usually explicitly labelled.
Scroll bars and arrows	Characteristics of a window that enable the user to move the contents of a window up or down.	Scrolling facilities can be provided through the use of cursor keys and function keys, or by clicking with a pointing device such as a mouse (see Table 4.4) on a scroll bar or arrow.
Screen buttons	Areas of the screen that will perform a function when selected.	Usually labelled boxes or circles. They perform a similar function to function keys but are activated by clicking with a pointing device such as a mouse.

Automatic scanners

There are a number of input devices that require little or no action by a user once the data have been recorded. These include hand-held data collection devices and portable computers in addition to a host of specialist input devices, such as scanners which check sheet metal for weak points. The more common automatic scanners are listed in Table 4.3.

Table 4.3 Automatic input devices

Device	Description	Key features
Bar code reader	Pen- or gun-like device that 'reads' black and white printed or magnetic bar codes when passed or held over them. Versions also exist that are embedded into work surfaces.	Suitable where the amount of data is limited and is not subject to rapid change (e.g. identification numbers such as product codes). Requires constant user operation with one or both hands. May also require one hand to hold the object.
Optical character reader (OCR)	Device that reads characters automatically.	Can handle a variety of data. Characters need to be well-formed (handwritten characters may be misinterpreted). No user involvement required once the documents have been positioned.
Document scanner	High-speed scanner that reads whole pages.	Used for inputting large amounts of text, diagrams and pictures.
Magnetic ink character recognition (MICR)	Device that interprets characters through the use of special ink.	As for OCR, but more reliable. Used mostly by banks (see the bottom of your cheque book).
Optical mark reader (OMR)	Device that detects the position of marks made on documents.	Specially designed forms are required so that the marks are correctly located. No user involvement is needed once the marks have been made.

Other input devices

Table 4.4 lists a variety of other input devices. These all have particular characteristics that make them more or less suitable for particular tasks. One important distinction is between discrete and continuous entry devices:

- *Discrete entry devices* allow the user to specify one of two states and are required where choice needs to be indicated.

- *Continuous entry devices* allow a user to vary infinitely the amount of information being input into the computer. The superiority of these input devices over a conventional keyboard when used to move a cursor or arrow around the screen has been demonstrated (Card *et al.*, 1978).

Some devices are predominantly continuous entry devices, but also include one or more facilities which permit discrete entry. For example, the mouse is a common continuous entry device which allows the cursor to be moved anywhere on the screen. Once it has been positioned, the mouse button is clicked to indicate that the object which is underneath the cursor should be selected. Many of the devices listed in Table 4.4 are normally used in conjunction with a keypad or other input device.

Table 4.4 Other input devices

Device	Description	Key features
Dataglove	Wired glove that apparently allows the wearer to grasp objects in three-dimensional space. See Figure 4.2 (page 64).	Used for manipulating objects and gesturing. The range of task possibilities is currently being explored.
Footmouse	A form of pedal that pivots. See Figure 4.3 (page 64).	The direction the pedal is moved in causes a cursor on the screen to move correspondingly. Suitable for 'coarse' movements. Leaves hands free for other tasks.
Gesture devices	Small transmitting device held by the user employed together with a receiving device associated with the computer.	The receiving device places the position and movement of the transmitting device in space. Facial gesture (expression) may be used in conjunction with speech systems for confirmation of requests.
Graphics tablet	Flat panel that is placed on a table near the computer display. The tablet surface represents the display.	Movement of a stylus or a finger across the surface causes a cursor to move across the screen or a line to be drawn. Very good for graphics input.

Table 4.4 (cont.)

Device	Description	Key features
Joystick	Small stick that can be moved in any direction within a fixed socket.	Often used for cursor-positioning tasks where precision is required. Requires a high level of concentration to use. Fine control is limited where fine grip is not possible.
Light pen	Pen that emits a light beam when a button is pressed.	Good for pointing and simple input. Has to be used against a vertical plane, so is not always very accurate. Difficult to use where grip is weak.
Mouse	Continuous input device that has one or more buttons for discrete input. Unlike the trackball or joystick it is not fixed, so the user can move it around on a flat surface.	The most common and popular of these devices. Highly versatile. May be optical, in which case a special pad must be used to track movement. Objects are manipulated by pressing control button(s) embedded in the mouse.
Pen and notepad	A pen is used with a small electronic notebook. Data can be entered using familiar techniques involving menus, forms and more innovative techniques.	The most impressive feature is the ability to input free-hand drawings and handwriting. However, the machine has to be taught to recognize the latter and most products can deal only with printed writing. Some gesture recognition may be possible.
Touch-sensitive screen or tablet	Special screen that detects the position of a finger touching it.	Relatively 'vandal-proof' and cannot be removed. Needs frequent cleaning. Very easy for people without any prior computer experience to use.
Trackball	Rotatable ball embedded in a surface in a fixed socket.	Can be moved by drawing the fingers or the palm of the hand over the surface or by flicking. Less force is required than for a joystick. Fast and does not require good grip for accurate use.
Video	Video camera and digitizer.	Necessary if video images are required.

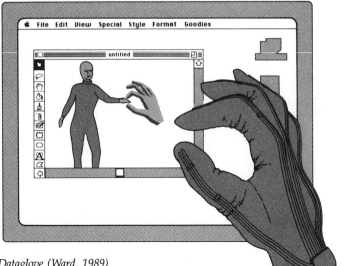

Figure 4.2   Dataglove (Ward, 1989)

Figure 4.3   Footmouse (Helander, 1988)

Speech

The thought of speaking to a computer has held appeal for some time and has been a focus of science fiction stories and films for many years. Details of speech input can be found in Oborne (1985), Waterworth (1988) or Booth (1989). Speech input suggests a number of advantages over other input methods:

- Since speech is a natural form of communication, training new users is much easier than with other input devices.

- Since speech input does not require the use of hands or other limbs, it enables operators to carry out other actions and to move around more freely.

- Speech input offers physically disabled people such as the blind or those with severe motor impairment the opportunities to use new technology.

However, speech input suffers from a number of problems:

- Speech recognizers have severe limitations. Whereas a human would have little problem distinguishing between similar-sounding words or phrases, speech recognition systems are likely to make mistakes.

- Speech recognizers are also subject to interference from background noise, although the use of a telephone-style handset or a headset may overcome this.

- Even if the speech can be recognized, the natural form of language used by people is very difficult for a computer to interpret (see Section 4.4).

- Because of this, speech input has been applied only in very specialized and highly constrained tasks.

Different speech input methods are summarized in Table 4.5.

Table 4.5 Speech recognition methods of input

Method	Description	Key features
Isolated word recognition	Can deal only with individual words.	Limited vocabulary. Pauses between words must be longer than normal. Users need training.
Continuous speech recognition	Can recognize words within strings of words.	Less limited vocabulary, but works by recognizing words from a continuous stream of speech. More prone to error than isolated word recognition systems but does not require special training of users.
Speaker-dependent	Can be used by individually identified speakers only.	System must 'learn' to recognize the speaker, who must 'train' the system. Easier to implement and more secure than speaker-independent systems, but may still have problems, e.g. if a speaker has a cold.
Speaker-independent	Attempts to deal with all users.	Attempts to deal with a wide range of vocal and speech characteristics. More difficult to implement and more prone to error than speaker-dependent systems.

Eye and head movement

The use of eye or head movement as input has similar advantages to speech in that it can be beneficial where a user's hands are disabled or otherwise occupied. If the computer can determine where the user is looking at any given time, it can present an input menu and then let the user select items by making a sound, pressing a button, squeezing a device, blowing, or pressing on a foot pedal. Methods of input using eye or head movement are summarized in Table 4.6.

Table 4.6 Eye and head movement methods of input

Method	Description	Key features
Electro-physiological sensing	Records muscle movement.	Electrodes have to be secured to the skin to detect muscle movement and are therefore subject to general body movement. May be uncomfortable and confining. Not well suited to the tracking of very small targets or to fine control.
Photo-electric reflection	Records movements in reflected light from the eye.	User must maintain a stable image on the central part of the retina. This is not easy to achieve. Not well suited to the tracking of very small targets or to fine control.
Head movement tracking	Lightweight headset, similar to a telephonist's, transmits ultrasonic signals to a measurement unit on top of the computer.	The 'keyboard' is a display on the screen of a computer. The system detects slight movements of the user's head and moves the cursor accordingly. To operate a key, the user locates the cursor on the key and then blows on a blow switch (a switch activated by a burst of air) in the headset 'mouth-piece'. This device can be used even by severely disabled people.

4.2   *Output*

Output devices are those devices that convert information coming from within a computer system into some form perceptible by a human. It is important to remember that output can be non-visual (for example, auditory) as well as visual.

Visual output

Visual output suits most people to some extent. However, it is unsuitable for tasks where visual attention has to be focused elsewhere (such as operating a machine or driving a vehicle). A significant proportion of the population suffer some visual impairment (such as near-sightedness, colour-blindness) and may find visual displays difficult to read. Bad lighting, eye fatigue, flickering screens and low quality of the displayed characters can all have a detrimental effect on visual output. Methods of visual output are summarized in Table 4.7.

Table 4.7 Visual output

Device	Key features
Microfiche or microfilm	Card-sized rectangle of film which records frames in a grid (fiche) or a continuous strip of film with frames, each frame equivalent to a sheet of paper. Suitable for longer-term storage of high-volume data. Requires magnifying readers and special equipment to make copies.
Plotter	Used for producing diagrams, maps and other precision continuous output. Can often produce coloured output through the use of different pens.
Printer	Many kinds available. Dot matrix and character printers vary greatly in quality of printing. Inkjet and laser printers offer high-quality output but may be expensive. Some provide colour.
Visual display unit (VDU)	VDUs vary in their ability to display colour and in the resolution and quality of the characters and graphics displayed. Some types of screen are not easily adaptable to graphics output or provide only one character type. Although high-resolution VDUs are more expensive, they can be considerably more beneficial to use.
Video	Video output is now becoming available and promises to have a big impact. For example, error messages and instructions can be issued by a video of a person talking to the user rather than by a cryptic message.

Non-visual output

The development of speech output devices has been very important in environments where visual displays would not be effective. Audio output is also vital for visually impaired people and can be very effective in providing feedback. For example, the sound of a disk 'chugging away' indicates that the system is doing something. Alarms can be used for attracting attention. Recently, audio output has been used to provide 'ear-cons'. These are audible icons, for

It's the instant answers I find hardest to deal with.'

example, a dragging sound when a graphic is dragged across the screen, a 'clunk' when something is put inside something else. The quality of speech output tends to be poor, limiting its use, but improvements are taking place rapidly. Methods of non-visual output are summarized in Table 4.8.

Table 4.8 Non-visual output

Type	Key features
Speech output: concatenation	Fragments of speech are recorded digitally and then re-assembled and played back to produce the desired words and sentences (Booth, 1989). Tends to be limited to applications requiring vocabularies of fewer than 200 words. Examples include the speaking clock and information such as details about changed telephone numbers and call diversions.
Speech output: synthesis-by-rule	Synthesis of words and sentences is controlled by rules of phonemics and rules that relate to the context of a sentence or phrase. Used in conjunction with a database, this method has the potential to produce a much larger range of responses than speech produced by concatenation. Pitch and tone can be varied but the speech produced can sound synthetic.
Electronic forms of output	Includes output on disk, digital transmission of messages and facsimile transmission direct from a computer.
Tactile output	Output using the sense of touch is of particular interest to blind users. Braille output is much bulkier than comparable printed output (Taylor *et al.*, 1990).

4.3 Screen design

The format and content of information displayed on the screen is very important in determining the success of a user's interaction with a system. If the information displayed is confusing or does not provide users with what they need, their performance will degrade. As illustrated in Section 2.2, simply organizing information in an easily accessible form can reduce dramatically the time taken to find a specific piece of information. It can also reduce error rates significantly.

The following guidelines for optimizing screen displays are based on Tullis (1988). For more on guidelines see Section 3.6.

Amount of information presented

A golden rule is to *minimize the total amount of information by presenting only what is necessary to the user.*

Techniques include the following:

- use concise wording

- use familiar data formats

- use tabular formats with column headings

- avoid unnecessary detail

- make *appropriate* use of abbreviations.

Grouping of information

Grouping similar items in a display together improves readability and can highlight relationships between different groups of data.

Techniques available include:

- colour coding (see section on colour on page 76)

- graphic borders around different groups of information (see Figure 4.4)

- highlighting using reverse video or brightness.

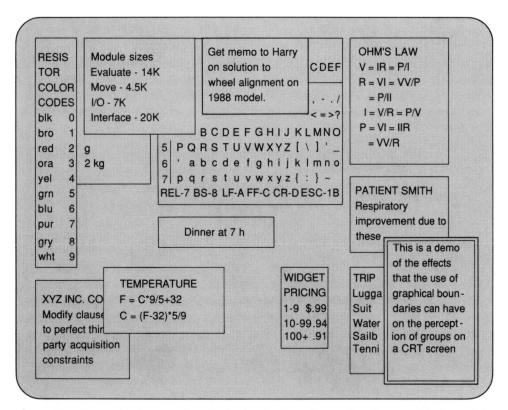

Figure 4.4   *Screen showing use of graphic borders to designate groupings (screen originally created using Tornado Notes (Micro Logic Corporation, Hackensack, NJ) for the IBM PC) (Tullis, 1988)*

Highlighting of information

At various stages of a task it is important to draw the user's attention to a specific piece of information. This can be achieved by:

- flashing
- reverse video
- underlining
- making the information bolder and brighter
- using a colour that stands out from the rest of the screen.

Standardization of screen displays

It is important to lay out screens in a way that will enable the users to know where to find a given piece of information. This is best achieved through using a consistent format for all the screens in an application (see Figure 4.5):

- Important information that needs attending to immediately should always be displayed in a prominent place to catch the user's eye.
- Information that is redundant should be displayed only if this facilitates the user's ability to process the information needed at that point of interaction.
- Reports and reference information should be grouped and displayed on the more peripheral areas of the screen.

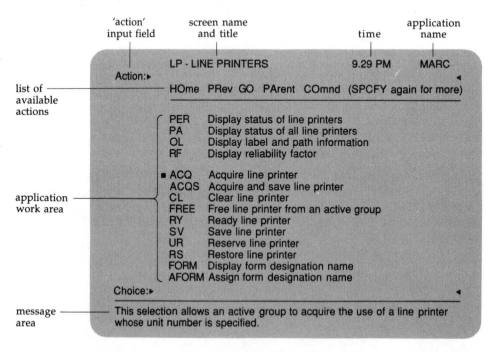

Figure 4.5 *Standard screen format for Burroughs 1986 InterPro™ series of mainframe software products (Tullis, 1988).*

Presentation of text

There are various guidelines concerned with text:

• Conventional upper and lower case text can be read about 13 per cent more quickly than text that is all upper case.

• Upper case characters are most effective for items that need to attract attention.

• Right-justified text, where the words have variable spacing, is more difficult to read than evenly spaced text with a ragged right margin.

• Optimal spacing between lines is equal to or slightly greater than the height of the characters themselves.

Graphics

Graphic representations play an important role in information display. For example, Table 4.9 shows a number of popular ways of presenting numeric data.

Table 4.9 Graphic techniques for representing numeric data

Graphic technique	Example	Usage notes
Scatterplots		Show how two continuous variables are correlated (or not), or show the distribution of points in two-dimensional space. Lines or curves may be superimposed to indicate trends.
Line graphs or curves		Show how two continuous variables are related to each other, especially changes in one variable over time. If time is included, it is typically plotted on the horizontal axis. A third, discrete, variable can be included using line-type or colour coding. Some designers recommend using no more than four lines (curves) per graph. When using multiple lines, each line should have an adjacent label.
Area, band, strata, or surface charts		Special type of graph that can be used when several line graphs or curves represent all the portions of a whole. The shaded areas stacked on top of each other represent each category's contribution to the whole. Least variable curves should be on the bottom and most variable on top to prevent 'propagation' of irregularities throughout stacked curves. Label the categories within the shaded areas.

Table 4.9 (cont.)

Graphic technique	Example	Usage notes
Bar graphs, column charts, or histograms	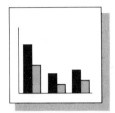	Show values of a single continuous variable for multiple separate entities, or for a variable sampled at discrete intervals. Adopt a consistent orientation (horizontal or vertical) for related graphs. Spacing between adjacent bars should typically be less than the bar width to facilitate comparisons between bars. A useful variation is the deviation bar chart, in which bars are constructed so that, under normal conditions, the bar ends lie in a straight line.
Pie charts		Show the relative distribution of data among parts that make up a whole. However, a bar or column chart will usually permit more accurate interpretation. If pie charts are used, some designers recommend using no more than five segments. Label the segments directly, and include the numeric values associated with the segments.
Simulated meters		Show one value of one continuous variable. When showing multiple values (i.e. multiple meters) that must be compared to each other, it is probably more effective to use other techniques, such as bar or column charts to show values for separate entities, or line graphs to show values changing over time.
Star, circular, or pattern charts		Show values of a continuous variable for multiple related entities. Values are displayed along spokes emanating from the origin. Different continuous variables may be represented if they are indexed so that the normal values of each variable can be connected to form an easily recognized polygon. Useful for detecting patterns, but not for determining precise values or making accurate comparisons among values.

(Adapted from Tullis, 1988)

The range of computer graphics available to designers increases year by year. Current graphics include line diagrams or solid shapes, which can be static or animated, two-dimensional or three-dimensional, monochrome or colour, and dynamic video images. In addition, graphics can be selected, moved, stretched, reduced or enlarged, and rotated. The designer must decide which of these options is most appropriate for the task in question.

Application and task domains that are most suited to being represented in graphic form at an interface include:

- those that require the user to make visual judgements (as in designing the spatial layout of circuit boards or buildings)

- those involving complex data systems (such as process control plant)

- numeric data which are multidimensional or constantly changing and from which the user has to detect trends and any defects

- direct manipulation interfaces and hypermedia systems.

Icons

Icons are small graphic images that are commonly used to represent different aspects of an interface metaphor (see Section 2.2). These aspects include system objects, options, operations, applications and messages. For example, as part of the desktop metaphor objects associated with working at an office desk (such as files, folders, printers) are depicted as icons (see Figure 4.6).

Typically, the user points to an icon and selects it. Further actions include *dragging* (moving) and opening. For example, an icon representing a document might be deleted by selecting it and then dragging it over the wastebasket icon.

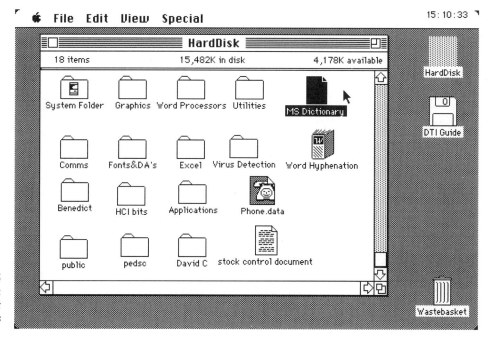

Figure 4.6 Macintosh™ screen showing different desktop icons

The advantage of icons compared with command names is that in many cases they are easier to learn and remember. They achieve this by:

- providing more visual information about the underlying object
- acting as powerful mnemonic cues
- explicitly showing the relationships between system objects.

When designing icons it is important to take into account:

- The *context* in which they are used. This is because the context influences the comprehensibility of the icons. For example, one reason why the meanings of the icons designed for the desktop metaphor are easily recognizable is that they represent objects within the specific context of the office environment. This reduces the possibility of misinterpretation.

- The *task domain* for which they are used. Some tasks are more suited to graphic representation. For example, tasks that require a user to discriminate between large amounts of information, such as filing and retrieval, can benefit from tagging the information with different types of icon.

- The *graphic form* that is used to depict the object. Icons can be concrete representations, abstract symbols or a combination of the two. In general, icons that are easiest to understand are those that combine both forms.

- The *nature of the underlying object* being represented. The more abstract the system concept, the more difficult it is to represent in iconic form.

- The extent to which one icon can be *discriminated* from other icons displayed. When there are a large number of icons it can be difficult to discriminate between them – especially when taking into account their small size. On the other hand, it is often the case that a number of system operations and objects share family relations (for example, delete a word, delete a paragraph, delete a page) which can be explicitly shown using common pictorial elements.

Colour

It seems highly likely that colour monitors will supersede monochrome monitors just as colour televisions have superseded black and white ones. The problem facing designers is how best to exploit colour to provide effective and pleasing screens.

- For graphics that are designed to resemble the *real world* – such as those developed for flight simulators or virtual realities (see Chapter 7) – it is desirable to use colours that resemble their everyday counterparts (blue for sky, green for grass).

- For systems that use *schematic representations* (for example, CAD, process control plant) it is preferable to capitalize on existing conventions (such as red for danger, green for go).

- For more *abstract representations* (like text or flowcharts) colour should be used more as a form of redundant coding, that is, an additional form of coding used alongside other types such as flashing or reverse video.

Colour can be very effective for:

- segmenting a display into separate regions
- search and detection tasks – particularly for inexperienced users
- enhancing the legibility of a colour symbol against its background.

However, colour should be used conservatively: too many colours clutter up the screen, increasing search times. Certain colour combinations, such as red on blue, should also be avoided, and the prevalence of colour-blindness should be borne in mind. For further information about the use of colour in HCI see Christ (1975) and Doney and Seton (1988).

The screen design process

As with any HCI design the approach to screen design should be dynamic, involving iterative evaluations of prototypes (see Chapters 5, 6 and 3). The guidelines suggested here should be taken as ground rules that can be adapted to the specific needs of an application. For a more comprehensive set of guidelines consult Tullis (1988) and Smith and Mosier (1986).

4.4   Communication styles

Dialogue refers to the exchange of instructions and information that takes place between a user and a computer system. Once the computer has been turned on, it issues a *prompt* (its request for input). The user then provides a *response* in which instructions or other data are specified in some form to the computer (the input). The instructions are interpreted by the computer and processing occurs. As a result the computer produces some output and the prompt and response cycle continues. The term *communication styles* covers all the ways that users interact with computer systems. Different styles are not mutually exclusive and it is likely that systems will use some combination.

Designing the dialogue and deciding on a style of communication are concerned not solely with how a system looks – the *representational* aspect. They are also concerned with how a system links sequences of operations together and maps the representations used on to its functions – these are the *operational* aspects. In communicating with the computer, users need to be aware of what they can do at each stage and what they have just done, that is, they need to be able to *navigate* through the system.

Command languages

Command languages were the typical communication style used by many early computers and they remain very common. Figure 4.7 (overleaf) shows an MS-DOS system in which the messages are cryptic. The > symbol is the prompt which indicates that the system is waiting to receive a command. Typing A: changes the current default disk drive to the A drive. Command languages require commands to be expressed using a precise syntax and so are intolerant of even the slightest syntactic errors.

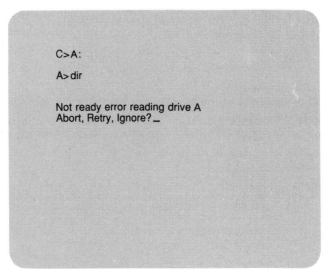

```
C>A:

A>dir


Not ready error reading drive A
Abort, Retry, Ignore?_
```

Figure 4.7   A dialogue using an MS-DOS system

In a command language system, the onus of navigation is on the user. The user has to know what the allowable commands are and needs to have a clear idea of the function to be performed. For the novice user this is clearly unsatisfactory, but for the expert it typically represents the quickest form of communication, particularly since commands may be expressed through the use of abbreviations or function keys (Section 4.1).

Menus

A menu is a prompt that consists of a limited set of options displayed on the screen. The user's response is to select one of the options. This results in some activity occurring. Unlike command-driven systems, therefore, in the case of menu-driven systems a user does not have to remember the name or abbreviation of a command, but only to recognize it from a list of options. Menus can therefore be helpful to learners.

Menus are often simple textual descriptions of the available functions. However, they can consist of icons, buttons displayed vertically or horizontally, or boxes which have to be 'ticked'. Indeed, any mechanism that allows for the selection from a limited set of options can be considered to be a menu. For menus to be effective, however, the names of the options, the contents of the icons or the descriptions of the buttons have to be self-explanatory, and this is not always the case. Often command keys are associated with menu items which provide a useful 'short-cut' for experienced users. Some menus are illustrated in Figure 4.8.

Menu systems require careful design and can become quite complex. The designer needs to consider:

- How to *order* menu items – alphabetically, by category, or by frequency (with the most frequently used options at the top). Some functions should be kept apart; for example, a 'create' option should not be next to a 'delete' option.

- How to *select* items from a menu – by typing a number or letter corresponding to the required option, by pointing at the option using a mouse or other pointing device, or by highlighting the item through cursor control keys.

- How to *navigate* through a series of menus. Many systems have hierarchically-structured menus where a user chooses from a main menu, is then presented with a series of sub-menus from which to make further selections, and so on until the required option is specified. If a user selects the wrong sub-menu the system should provide an easy way of returning to the previous level.

There are four main types of menu:

- *Fixed menus* remain in place until the option is chosen.

- *Pull-down menus* are dragged down from a single title (or menu bar) at the top of the screen, an item is selected, and the menu automatically returns back to its original title. (See Figure 4.8(a).)

- *Pop-up menus* appear when a user clicks on a particular area of screen, which may be designated by an icon. The menu remains in position until the user instructs it to disappear again, usually by clicking on a 'close box' in the border of the menu's window.

- *Walk-through* or *cascading menus* display all the options chosen one after the other. (See Figure 4.8(b).)

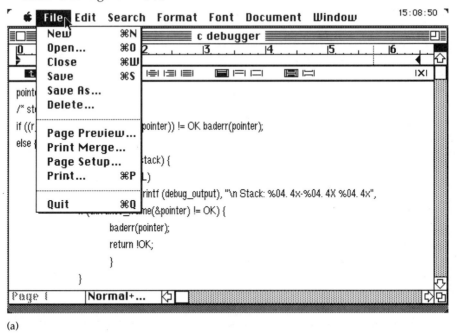

*Figure 4.8
Types of menu:
(a) a Microsoft®
Word pull-down
menu and
alternative
commands on the
Apple® Macintosh™;
(b) walk-through
menus*

Natural language dialogue

The use of ordinary language as a means of communicating with a computer has been considered highly desirable because of its naturalness. However, the fact that the system needs to be able to cope with the vagueness, ambiguity and ungrammatical constructions associated with natural language has proved a stubborn problem for artificial intelligence research, and currently there are no truly natural language systems.

All current natural language systems are in fact pseudo-natural language systems which handle only a limited subset of a language, frequently simply providing more natural synonyms for obscure command names. Ideally, a natural language dialogue would be spoken, but speech recognition is still imperfect (Section 4.1). Pseudo-natural language dialogues therefore require the text to be typed in, which brings its own problems of spelling errors and slow, long-winded input. Because of this, users tend to use shorter and shorter abbreviations until their 'natural' language dialogue finishes up as a personalized command language! Although natural language promises flexible and easy communication with computers, most natural language systems developed in the foreseeable future will be limited to well-defined domains using a limited vocabulary.

Question and answer dialogues

Question and answer dialogues can be used when the expected input is constrained by the domain and when an option is dependent on the previous option chosen. The system prompts with a question to which the user responds by a simple yes or no answer or by selecting from a menu. Question and answer dialogues are *system-driven* dialogues which protect the user from any considerations of navigation. Therefore, they are suitable for novice users, but can be very frustrating for experienced users who know what they want to do.

Form-filling

When several different categories of data are to be fed into a system using a keyboard, it is often helpful to design the screen to look like a form. This is particularly suitable when the same type of data has to be entered repeatedly, as in retailing (type, number, price, stock, delivery) and other data processing applications. One way of making forms easy to use is to design them so that they are similar in appearance to well-designed paper forms. Form-filling is often used in conjunction with a menu-style interface. Figure 4.9 (opposite) illustrates a form-filling dialogue.

Direct manipulation

The term *direct manipulation* was first coined by Shneiderman (1983) to describe systems that feature:

- Visibility of the objects of interest. This is usually accomplished by representing the object by an icon (see Section 4.3).

- Rapid, reversible, incremental actions.

> Type in the information below,
> pressing TAB to move the cursor, and
> press ENTER when done.
>
> Name: _____ Phone: (____) ____ - ____
> Address: _____
> _____
> City: _____ State: _____ Zip Code: _____
> Charge Number: __ __ __ __ __
>
> | Catalog Number | Quantity | Catalog Number | Quantity |
> |---|---|---|---|
> | _____ | _____ | _____ | _____ |
> | _____ | _____ | _____ | _____ |
> | _____ | _____ | _____ | _____ |
> | _____ | _____ | _____ | _____ |
> | _____ | _____ | _____ | _____ |

Figure 4.9   A form-fill design for a department store (Shneiderman, 1987)

- Direct manipulation of the object of interest instead of complex command language syntax. For example, to copy a file called FileX from a disk in disk drive A to a disk in drive B, the icon representing FileX is physically moved from the icon representing the disk in drive A to the icon representing the other disk. In a command language the same function would be achieved by typing in (for example) COPY A:FileX B:

Portrait of interactivity

Typically, direct manipulation systems are characterized by:

- *windows* to divide the screen into areas
- *icons* representing objects which can be moved around the screen
- a *mouse* (or other pointing device) which manipulates objects on the display
- *pop-up or pull-down menus* which display the options available.

Because of this arrangement, direct manipulation systems are often known as WIMP interfaces (*w*indows, *i*cons, *m*ouse or *m*enus, *p*op-up or *p*ull-down menus or *p*ointing). Figure 4.10 illustrates a typical WIMP interface. WIMP interfaces are now widely available on most computers and offer many benefits over other communication styles. In particular:

- The whole of a system is easily visible because objects are represented by icons and the available menu options can be inspected by pulling down menus.
- The basic actions (e.g. opening, closing, copying, deleting, scrolling) are consistent across systems. This makes learning new systems much easier.
- Exploration of the system is facilitated because any action can be 'undone' (reversed) if it does not have the required effect.

More recently another term, 'graphical user interface' (GUI), has come into use to describe interfaces which, as well as having these characteristics, are also strongly graphical – as the name suggests. Well-designed GUIs appear to be easy for novices to use for some tasks but as yet the psychological reasons for this are poorly understood (Furnas, 1991).

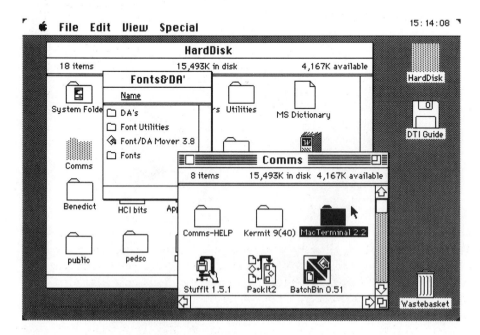

Figure 4.10   Example of a WIMP interface

4.5   User support

Users require considerable support in order to help them learn what a system can do and to improve their performance and understanding. User support can be provided through:

• *online-based support tools* such as tutorials, help and online manuals

• *documentation*

• *training* and *advice*.

Online-based support

Online *tutorials* have become popular as a means of helping beginners to get started. The tutorials commonly take the form of a 'guided tour' through the facilities of a system. However, often learners are required to practise tasks that are unrelated to the actual work they are to perform, and so may abandon tutorials to strike out on their own and indulge in learning through doing (Carroll and Mack, 1984). Although this may be satisfactory, and indeed is facilitated by WIMP interfaces, it may result in the users learning only a subset of the available system functions (Carroll *et al.*, 1985).

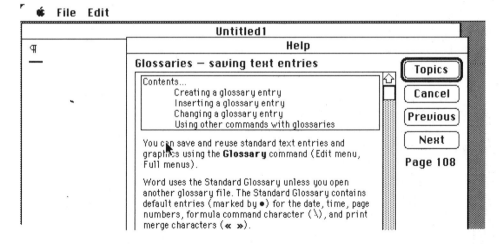

Figure 4.11   Help window

Online *help systems* or online manuals are a popular means of providing continuing support once a user has achieved a measure of expertise and become independent. Help systems provide quick and easy (usually) menu-based access to the system documentation and the more advanced systems allow some user tailoring of the level of help. For example, an expert may need only a cursory reminder about the use of some function, whereas a novice may require an extensive explanation. Some help systems provide *context-sensitive help* which allows a user to obtain help on the particular command that she is using.

'Think back ... which keys did you press?'

Another area which can be helpful in giving user support is *computer-assisted instruction (CAI)* and its closely related variants, CBT (computer-based training) or CAL (computer-aided learning). These systems provide a variety of examples, descriptions, questions and solutions about a system (and are not limited to describing computer systems). CAI systems can be particularly useful when thoroughly new concepts are introduced.

Elkerton (1988) advocates improving online aids by following the design principles below:

- Describe what can be done in terms of the task.
- Give the user the power to adjust the level of detail, thus accommodating a wide range of users.
- Make advice procedurally incomplete, as this will assist active learning.
- Provide feedback to remind users of appropriate procedures to use, particularly when recovering from errors.
- Develop modular assistance and instructional dialogues to describe similar and dissimilar procedures.

Document-based support

Computer documentation has many purposes and forms. It ranges from how to assemble hardware to general advice on getting the best from software. It can be in the form of an introductory tutorial, a detailed technical manual or a quick reference guide intended for expert users. Most documentation is paper-based, but can include audio-tapes, videos and dynamic computer displays. Overviews and summaries are also found to be helpful.

There is evidence to suggest that minimizing information by using summaries only can be extremely helpful. The *'minimal manual'* (Carroll *et al.*, 1988b; Carroll, 1990) emphasizes learning by doing and encourages interaction. This approach can be coupled very effectively with online *'micro worlds'* where a user can safely try out various procedures and strategies.

As with any other part of an interface, documentation needs to be designed and developed iteratively using evaluation. It is difficult to anticipate what problems users will have with an interface and therefore in what situations they will need documentation and what type of documentation they will need. This information can be ascertained only during an integrated process of development of both the interface and its documentation.

Instructor-based and expert-based support

Support for users within organizations varies widely. It may range from informal reference to a 'local expert' (someone in the organization who has become accomplished with a system) to a group of designated experts responsible for user support, training and help. The *information centre* approach to system development establishes a central department which advises and assists users to develop their own systems. This is now being adopted by many organizations and can help considerably with the provision of expertise.

Courses are available from higher education establishments and commercial concerns on either a face-to-face or a distance learning basis, and they provide an excellent form of in-depth education on general techniques or specific pieces of software. Software suppliers often provide telephone help lines (or 'hot-lines') to deal with detailed queries.

Expert-based help is often regarded as a form of emergency service – it is intended to help out users who are experiencing problems that they cannot deal with themselves. The effectiveness of this type of help depends greatly on the expert involved, particularly in in-house arrangements where the person on the help-desk may not have chosen to be there, and may therefore resent the task and may be unhelpful. Few experts are also trained to be helpful; they have a tendency to solve the problem without using the opportunity to extend the user's knowledge or understanding. Although this 'trouble-shooting' approach appears effective, good education and training have longer-term benefits.

4.6 Types of system

Interface designers have to weigh up the important factors of a system in order to select the input and output devices, screen displays, communication style and type of user support that is most suitable for the tasks to be performed and the environment in which the system must operate. An appropriate solution for one system may be quite inadequate for another.

Example

Computer-aided design and computer-aided manufacturing systems (CAD/CAM) assist the analyst or designer of two-dimensional and three-dimensional artefacts. They typically provide a variety of facilities for experimenting with designs and manipulating two-dimensional and three-dimensional images. With typical CAD/CAM systems:

- *Users* may be expected to be well-educated, skilled and willing to devote energy to mastering a computer system.

- The *tasks* that they are doing are well-understood and well-defined, although technically complex.

- The *environment* will be safe and calm, with no great pressure for a particularly fast response from the computer.

- *User support* will be provided by manuals, although there may be some human support.

- *Output* will require high-resolution graphic displays and there may be a need for special printers or plotters.

- *Input* will demand extremely precise input mechanisms which facilitate continuous input.

- *Communication style* will be user-driven, probably using direct manipulation techniques.

Example

Automatic teller machines (ATM) – the 'hole in the wall' – used by most high street banks allow members of the public to obtain cash from their accounts and to perform other simple banking functions. In these systems:

- *Users* will approach the system with a whole host of attitudes – perhaps a desire to 'outdo' the machine, a desire to complete the transaction as soon as possible, or a dread of touching the machine! Many of the users will be unfamiliar with other computer systems, they cannot be expected to be familiar with a keyboard or other input devices, and they will range widely in age, experience and physical abilities.

- *Tasks* are limited to a few basic banking functions, but the users may not be aware of the tasks available or of the structure of those tasks. Tasks must be kept simple and must be carefully structured. Originally, ATMs dispensed cash before releasing the customer's card, but in most systems nowadays users are forced to remove the card *before* the machine gives out any money. This simple change in task structure overcomes the problem of people getting their money (and, from their perspective, completing the task) and forgetting the card.

- The *environment* must ensure that the system is secure. The screen will regularly become dirty and greasy. A user may feel pressured to complete a transaction quickly if there is a lengthy queue. The system has to operate out-of-doors.

- *User support* is limited to the instructions provided by the machine and perhaps any brochure which accompanies the bank card.

- The amount of data to be *input* must be very limited (since users cannot be expected to be able to type). A numeric keypad is generally all that is required, coupled with a few labelled function keys.

- *Output* must be concise and easy to understand, and is limited by the size of screen.

- *Communication style* will be system-driven, based around menu selection, a question and answer dialogue and sometimes use of hard keys, for example, keys labelled with specific amounts of money (£50, £100, etc.).

Table 4.10 (overleaf) illustrates some of the issues involved for six different types of system in terms of the tasks to be performed, the environment and relevant user support.

Table 4.10 Features of different types of system

Systems	Users	User support	Environment and tasks
Office systems. Examples: database systems, spreadsheets, management information systems, decision support systems.	Users can be expected to devote effort to learning the basics of the technology if it is central to their work. Some discretionary and intermittent users. Users can be expected to have basic keyboard skills and/or be familiar with other input devices.	Support available from colleagues. Likely to be a 'local expert'. Plenty of documentation and manuals. Telephone 'hot-lines' available free to the user in distress.	(Relatively) calm. Rarely a requirement for an instantaneous response from the computer – a response time in the order of one or two seconds is adequate for most purposes. Tasks are generally well-defined and well-understood.
Public information systems or walk-up-and-use systems. Examples: automatic teller machines (ATMs), public information databases, home tele-shopping, automatic ticket machines.	Members of the public who have a wide variety of skills, knowledge and capabilities. Many intermittent, discretionary and casual users. Users may not possess keyboard skills, mouse skills or other specific interaction techniques. Disadvantaged users must be catered for.	Little opportunity to provide user support. Users cannot be expected to read large amounts of documentation before using the system. Rarely a 'local expert' to help.	Highly variable environment in terms of cost, ease of access and time constraints. Tasks may be difficult to determine especially with increasingly open systems (i.e. large networks of interconnected systems).
Knowledge-based systems (KBSs). Examples: planning systems, diagnostic systems, natural language (NL) systems, advice-giving systems.	Users may be experts in their field, using an expert system to help in decision-making and hence can be expected to devote energy to learning the system. Alternatively, users may be novices in the field seeking to obtain expertise, and hence may be more casual users.	Usually access is provided to plenty of on-line help and other user support. The documentation may be difficult to understand because of the size of these systems. Little general expertise available. In-depth training courses may be needed for first-time users.	Typically tasks are complex and may be poorly understood. Systems need to *explain* their reasoning to convince users. Environment either as for office systems or as for public information systems.

Table 4.10 (cont.)

Systems	Users	User support	Environment and tasks
Complex, real-time systems. Examples: control systems used in civilian and military aircraft, large plant processing and monitoring systems (e.g. nuclear power stations, chemical processing, oil-rigs), missile and rocket guidance systems. Known as safety-critical systems where safety is paramount.	Users typically highly trained. Have to monitor many aspects of the systems simultaneously. Have to deal with the demands of real-time control. No discretionary or casual users.	Should be good, but may be highly complex. General support unlikely to be available. Considerable training required to be used effectively.	Both highly complex. Many things may be happening extremely quickly. May require novel input and output devices. Complex and non-standard data. Tasks are difficult to analyse and accurately define. Demands of real-time working.
Computer supported co-operative work (CSCW). Examples: electronic mail (e-mail), electronic conferencing systems, electronic meetings or electronic phone systems, joint authoring systems.	Many casual and novice users. Likely to be many discretionary users as other methods of working offer alternatives.	After initial training, on-line support must be available. Co-operative setting may provide 'local expert' assistance.	Heterogeneous computer systems may be unable to 'communicate' with each other (due to 'translation' problems). Need for private work spaces as well as public ones. Tasks still being explored, e.g. distributed project management and decision support.
Hypermedia systems. In contrast to conventional database systems these systems have many nodes containing information displayed via different media linked together. Example: flexible information systems with a much higher degree of user control than conventional database systems. Two closely related systems are hypertext and multimedia. Hypertext systems contain multi-branching text and diagrams. Multimedia systems are collections of media with few branching points. The terms multimedia and hypermedia are often used synonymously.	Typical users will not be computer experts. Users determine their own paths through the information by deciding which links to follow. The major problem for users is navigation: knowing where they are, where they want to go, how to get there, where they have been and what else there is to see.	Navigation through the data (often known as 'hyperspace') can be a major problem. Well-chosen metaphors and good online support can help to improve usability. For example, providing maps showing the user's position, guides who answer questions, guided tours, trails and book-marks, etc. are well-known techniques for helping users to orientate themselves.	Most tasks involve finding information and/or learning. Typically users browse or search large collections of graphic material (e.g. fine art collections, tourist and encyclopedia information) or learn concepts and skills. The majority of systems are located in educational establishments, museums and exhibitions, etc.

Any computer program used to design, make, maintain, manage or test a software product can be called a software tool. Software tools are programs that support designers and programmers at some point in the development of a software product. The availability of software tools makes it possible to prototype systems, and indeed the desire to prototype has influenced the properties of the tools.

Virtually everything that an interface designer does can be supported – to a greater or lesser degree – by the provision of software tools. The term 'software tool' often conjures up the idea of an extremely complex piece of software. In reality it may be anything from a routine that controls the movement of a mouse to a software system which helps in the scheduling and control of entire projects. In general, we may say that a software tool provides a number of *facilities* or *utilities* for a system developer. Sometimes the term *package* is used to emphasize that a tool includes a number of facilities.

5.1   The need for software tools

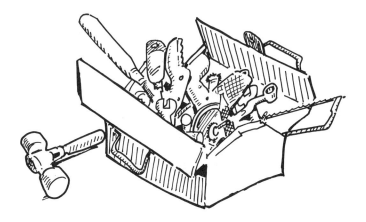

Each stage of a system life-cycle (Section 3.1) – planning, requirements analysis and specification, systems design, implementation, evaluation and operations and maintenance – can be improved through the provision of software tools. The term *computer-aided software engineering* (*CASE*) describes the software tools that support the software engineering process. Those tools supporting analysis and design are sometimes known as 'front-end CASE', and those supporting the implementation, operation and maintenance of systems as 'back-end CASE'. CASE tools provide three main benefits:

- increased productivity
- enhanced software quality
- easier and better management of software development.

Tools are needed to support all aspects of systems development. Recent recognition of the importance and difficulty of interface design has prompted the development of many tools to help the interface designer. One important feature of interface design is the separation of an interface from the underlying functionality of a system. An interface designer has to consider:

- *What a system can do.* This involves consideration of both the *functionality* of a system and the *structure* of the objects that constitute the system.

- *How it does it.* This covers the *operational* aspects of the system, that is, what actions have to be undertaken, and in what sequence, in order to perform the functions.

- *What it will look like.* This is the *representational* aspect of a system; it describes the form and content of the dialogue (Section 4.4) and the design and layout of objects on the screen (Section 4.3).

- *What assistance is available.* This means the *user support* provisions in the form of help messages, error handling and alternative interfaces for different users (Section 4.5).

CASE is big business. A recent estimate identified 600 different CASE tools on the market. Yet very few data processing professionals recognize the importance of CASE (Downes *et al.*, 1991). The bewildering array of tools and the often exaggerated claims for what they can do may contribute to this situation. However, this jungle of terminology can be tamed by identifying two main categories of tool:

- *General-purpose, stand-alone tools.* These are tools that perform generalized functions, for example, word processors, drawing packages and programming languages. There is a wide range of flexibility in these tools.

- *Integrated environments or 'tool kits'.* These are coherent sets of tools aimed at a specific part of systems development work. Many environments also help with the operation, maintenance and management of systems and provide functions to create and revise a system, ensure consistency, maintain its integrity and quality and monitor its usage.

5.2   General-purpose tools

The flexibility of general-purpose tools is their strength. However, if they are to be used successfully the system developer must be aware of their relative strengths and weaknesses. Within the category of general-purpose tools, it is possible to identify:

- languages and related tools
- text manipulation tools
- graphics tools
- modelling and diagramming tools.

Languages and related tools

A host of languages is available for defining and manipulating a variety of objects. Although programming languages are some of the most flexible of tools, flexibility usually comes with a price – the need for expertise. Languages are usually accompanied by a number of related tools that assist the writing and testing of programs. Some major types of language and related tool are illustrated in Table 5.1.

Table 5.1 Languages and related tools

Language or tool	Features and uses
Third generation languages (3GLs), e.g. COBOL, Pascal, FORTRAN	Procedural languages. Programmers have to deal with details of the sequence of program operations. Widely available, widely used.
	Primarily oriented towards the production of reports. Often provide little screen handling. Require time and expertise to write and test programs.
Re-usable software	*Modules* (general limited-purpose programs) are gathered into *libraries*. Modules from the same or different libraries are linked together into a program and can be re-used any number of times. For example, the same module may move the cursor on a number of different video displays.
	Libraries are commercially available for both programming functions and displays. See also graphics environments (Section 5.3).
Fourth generation languages (4GLs): many proprietary brands available	Less procedural than 3GLs. 4GLs provide enhanced screen handling facilities and are easier to write and test than 3GLs. Often capable of generating 3GL code (program generators).

Table 5.1 (cont.)

Language or tool	Features and uses
Fourth generation languages (4GLs): many proprietary brands available	Good for prototyping and quick production of working systems. Used with screen painters and report generators (Table 5.3) they become application generators which generate a system from a 4GL description. 4GLs can be used by end-users. May impose too many restrictions on what can be done for some applications.
Fifth generation languages (5GLs)	Expected to incorporate artificial intelligence techniques. Systems now available couple production rule programming, functional programming and/or OOP (see opposite) with 4GL capabilities.
Very high level languages (VHLL), e.g. APL, LISP and Prolog	Allow complicated operations to be expressed in very little code. Quick to write. May have poor screen handling. Limited for end-user use. Expressive, usually interpretive and interactive and often with good programming environments. All these characteristics contribute to their suitability for prototyping, particularly system functionality. May use a lot of memory and be uneconomic for the implementation of a final system.
Data manipulation languages (DML), e.g. SQL	Highly non-procedural languages associated with database systems. Free the programmer from details of navigation. Excellent for prototyping content of reports and displays before layout is considered. Typically little screen handling. May be coupled with 4GLs.
Functional languages, e.g. SASL, ML, Miranda	Programs are smaller and easier to produce than with 3GLs. Used as a part of 5GL approach. Uses still to be explored in detail.

Table 5.1 (cont.)

Language or tool	Features and uses
Object-oriented programming (OOP), e.g. SmallTalk™	Concentrates on the definition of the attributes and behaviour of objects. An object is a collection of data together with modules (called operations or methods) for accessing these data.
	Objects group data and operations into a coherent unit. Particularly important in interface design to describe interface objects such as icons, windows and active images (Table 5.3).
Hypermedia systems, e.g. HyperCard®, Guide, SuperCard®	Useful as prototyping tools for interactive systems. Low cost, easily obtainable and attaining a high standard of software quality. The appearance of an interactive system is very easy to prototype in HyperCard® provided that the structure of the display is fairly simple. Buttons and text fields are fairly general-purpose, integrated input–output objects that are adequate for even relatively complex applications.
Programming by example	Typified by the way that robots are 'taught' (i.e. programmed) to perform certain functions. The programmer leads the robot through a typical example procedure, and the robot records the actions taken.
	Applications are being explored in office systems. May have a big impact particularly for end-user development, but as yet the applications are limited.
Authoring languages and tools	Provide a number of facilities for describing screen layouts and conditional branching mechanisms.
	Tools are also available for direct video capture. For example, using QuickTime™ and other associated tools, users can edit and insert movie clips, animated graphics, stills and sound into their programs.
Event–response or rule-based languages	Based on the IF *condition* THEN *action* construct. Easy to write but can become complex.
	Particularly relevant to expert systems, but are also used extensively in programming active images (Table 5.3) and other OOP systems.

Table 5.1 (cont.)

Language or tool	Features and uses
Access-oriented and data-directed programming	Special data values (called cells, active values or demons) exist that are constantly active and can notify other parts of a system when they are accessed or changed.
	Used with active images (Table 5.3) access-oriented programming offers a very powerful facility for prototyping and implementing graphic interfaces.
Browsers	Provide navigation facilities which enable the user to move rapidly through a program, graphic, database or other environment locating specific objects. Browsers often include facilities for moving, copying, opening and closing objects, zooming in on a portion of a graphic or panning out to get a better perspective.
	Other browsing facilities will show the user's current location in the program and the sequence of objects that have been accessed. This is particularly important in hypermedia systems, where it is very easy to get lost without these navigational aids.
Debugging tools	Provide a variety of facilities for showing traces of a program's behaviour, which pieces of code have been executed, what the values of variables are, and so on. Displays can be made at different points and programs can be altered quickly and re-run immediately.

Text manipulation tools

Text manipulation tools vary from the humble text editor to desktop publishing systems, and they are vital for almost every application. The main types are described in Table 5.2. However, when there is a requirement for elegant typography, text manipulation will not be adequate.

Table 5.2 Text manipulation tools

Tool	Features and uses
Text editors	Developed to help with entering and amending program statements. Structured editors are designed to be used with specific programming languages and reflect the particular structure of those languages.
Word processors	Provide a range of facilities for entering, changing and laying out text. Have continually matured and now provide many facilities related to producing text such as spell-checking and outlining. More advanced versions also incorporate graphics capabilities.
Desktop publishing systems (DTP) or document processing systems	Enhanced word processors. Have additional facilities coupled with enhanced quality of printing, variety of font sizes and styles and details of layouts. Facilitate laying out pages and documents. The very advanced systems verge on electronic publishing (EP) systems as used by newspapers and publishing businesses.

Graphics tools

Graphics tools allow interface designers to create and manipulate drawings, icons and other graphic images. Designers need to be able to lay out windows (variable sized regions of the screen) and displays which are composed of display objects such as text, lines, shapes and icons. Designers may also want to create other graphic objects such as buttons, dials, cursors, sliders, scroll bars, bubbles, highlightable menu items and so on.

In addition to simply designing layout – the *representational* aspects – an interface designer must link the screens, images and text to the functions of the system, and sequence the images in order to describe *operational aspects* of an interface. These determine what it is that makes one interactive session different from another and give a user interface its 'look and feel' as much, if not more, than the physical presentation of a display. Graphics tools are described in Table 5.3.

Table 5.3 Graphics tools

Tool	Features and uses
Icon editors	Facilitate the creation of icons (pictures) and the manipulation of these through reshaping, resizing, rotating and so on.
Menu builders	Allow the rapid creation of menu structures. Menus may be textual, but can also appear as labelled boxes in a vertical or horizontal layout.
Window managers	Enable the production of windows of varying and variable size and shape. Also support the manipulation of windows by the end-user so that they can be moved around the screen, hidden behind one another, overlap each other and so on.
Drawing packages	Group graphic primitives such as circles, rectangles and lines of various dimensions into display objects. Offer other capabilities such as shading in different styles. From these primitives, designers can create intricate drawings which can also be rotated, moved, stretched and shrunk.
Painting packages	Use a bit-map representation of rectangular portions of a display which can be moved over each other, inverted or combined. Similar facilities to drawing packages.

Table 5.3 (cont.)

Tool	Features and uses
Menu systems	Provide facilities to link menu items together and attach them to system functions.
Screen painters	Enable the designer to lay out an entire screen such as an input 'form' (Section 4.4).
	Fields on the screen can be defined as input and/or output and can have various attributes such as reverse video or highlighting. Fields can also be tailored to accept only particular data types.
Report generators	Provide facilities similar to screen painters for producing printed or displayed reports. Provide additional facilities such as the production of totals, page headings and summaries.
Active processes or active images	Allow images on a screen to be connected to the underlying functions of a system. Used with access-oriented and data-directed programming (Table 5.1). For example, a graphic image of a dial will always accurately reflect the value of the datum to which it is attached. Changing the datum will automatically change the appearance of the dial. Similarly, changing the graphic image will change the underlying datum value.

Modelling and diagramming tools

Graphics tools allow things to be drawn and text manipulation tools perform simple text processing. Modelling tools can be either graphically based or text based, but in addition to drawing or text manipulation they also check and maintain the syntax and semantics of a model. This gives the benefit that code can be produced directly from a syntactically correct model.

'Every now and then I let it do a self-portrait.'

Example

In a drawing package, drawing a line connecting two boxes has no intrinsic meaning whereas in a modelling tool it may mean that data can flow between objects represented by one box to another. With a drawing tool if a box is moved on the screen, the line will move with it only if the box and line have been grouped together. With a modelling tool the line will automatically move (and be shrunk, extended or reshaped as necessary) in order to maintain a semantic link. Modelling tools also check that a model conforms to any in-house standards or rules of a specific methodology.

Graphically-based models, or diagrams, tend to be simpler to produce and easier to understand than text-based models. However, complex diagrams are still notoriously difficult to draw and maintain, particularly if they are large. Automating the diagramming process overcomes this problem. Unfortunately, many of the models used for interface design are not graphically based, but are text based. Moreover, many of the design techniques discussed in Section 3.3 do not have any software support at all. For example, there are no CLG, TAG, GOMS or keystroke modellers. Although there is some support for BNF-style grammars, production rule representations and other formal methods (Yourdon and Constantine, 1979), the specification of dialogues – and direct manipulation dialogues in particular – using these methods is complicated and hence liable to error. Table 5.4 describes the principal modelling tools that are available.

Table 5.4 Modelling tools

Tool	Features and uses
Data flow diagrammers	Allow the production of data flow diagrams (DFDs) that show the flow of data among processes, sources, destinations and data stores.
Concept modelling tools	Model the concepts, or objects in a system and the relationships between them.
Transition network modellers	Represent the methods of moving from one system state to another. Particularly useful for designing dialogue sequencing.
Structure charts	Used for a variety of purposes where a hierarchical structure occurs.
User modelling tools	User modelling has been suggested as both an aid to design and a component in an adaptive system or intelligent interface. Characteristics of the possible users of a system are represented either to assist a designer or to be accessed directly by a system, which eventually builds a model of the preferences, style and knowledge of each individual user.

5.3   Integrated environments

There are a number of problems with using general-purpose, stand-alone tools:

- Transferring data between tools can be very difficult and time-consuming. Even where tools provide a transfer facility, details of formatting and structuring can be lost in the process.

- One or more facilities may be inadequate. For example, the text processing facilities in a drawing package may not be as good as those in a word processor.

- There may be lack of consistency among tools. There is also likely to be a lack of consistency across interfaces which means that a 'house style' and internal interface standards cannot easily be enforced.

As a result of these problems, there has been a move away from stand-alone tools to integrated environments which are also referred to as tool kits, system shells, management systems or environments.

Integrated environments can be expected to provide a number of facilities over and above those offered by their constituent tools. Possible facilities include:

- *Configuration management.* It should be possible to set up or configure an integrated environment to reflect any in-house standards or methodology.

- *Version control.* Controlling different versions of programs, screens and other objects in a system is vital to ensure good quality (for example, an untested version of a system object cannot replace a well-tested one) and can become very complex.

- *A coherent body of knowledge about the system itself, for example a data dictionary.* Such a body of knowledge is necessary for version control, but it is also invaluable for ensuring consistency and unambiguous communication between system developers.

- *Accommodation of other tools.* There is a danger in becoming tied to a single environment and much effort has recently gone into establishing a standard for common interfaces so that environments can accommodate new tools as they are released or as the organization requires them. This standard is referred to as the public tools interface (PTI) or the public common tools interface (PCTI). PTI has now been implemented as the portable common tools environment (PCTE) (Campbell, 1987). Standards exist for windowing systems, graphics environments and so on (Section 3.6).

Not all these facilities will be provided by any one environment. Some are oriented towards supporting design, others to implementation and others to operation and maintenance. The main environments are considered below. However, the following general points about integrated environments should not be overlooked:

- An operating system is an integrated environment providing a range of basic facilities for file management, access control, and so on.

- Often an operating system is combined with compilers, interpreters, debuggers and so on, and becomes a programming or software engineering environment.

- Graphics environments integrate graphics tools (often with an operating system and programming environment) and libraries of graphics modules (see Table 5.1). The most notable of these environments is probably the MacTools™ environment which comes with all Macintosh™ computers and gives them their distinctive 'look and feel' (Apple® Computer, 1987). Other environments are available on Xerox workstations and Sun systems. For windowing PCs, there are commercial libraries like GEM® and Microsoft® Windows.

Most of these are the low-level environments that are exploited primarily by programmers. For system designers and end-users there are a number of integrated development and operational environments which sit on top of these and exploit their facilities.

Analyst's workbenches

An analyst's workbench (AWB) is a collection of 'front-end' CASE tools that support a system analyst's and designer's work. Almost invariably, an AWB is built around providing support for a particular methodology, such as SSADM (Downes *et al.*, 1991), Yourdon (Yourdon and Constantine, 1979) or information engineering (Martin, 1986). Different methodologies prefer different styles of tools, but all use the basics of a dataflow diagram, a conceptual modelling tool and some form of structure chart.

AWBs can significantly improve productivity and enhance quality and consistency. AWBs always have a data dictionary facility as a central component. Many generate code automatically which can then be run under a common operating system. Some AWBs produce data descriptions as well so that systems can be run using the facilities of a particular database management system.

Some AWBs go beyond providing tools to help the analyst and include facilities to help in the planning phase of project development in addition to the production phase. Such a system is known as an *integrated project support environment* (*IPSE*). IPSEs integrate project management functions with an analyst's tool kit. They also provide facilities to deal with change. Particularly in the case of large systems, requirements change and these new developments must be costed, scheduled and monitored. IPSEs therefore seek to offer a method of controlling the entire life-cycle of systems development. In order to cope with this variety, they must offer a PTI.

User interface management systems (UIMSs)

A UIMS is software intended for the development and use of user interfaces. The main objective of a UIMS is to free interface designers from low-level interface details and provide them with a comprehensive set of tools. A UIMS essentially consists of three complementary parts:

- a *graphics and text environment* including window, screen and menu design facilities (media tools)

- a *linkage function* that defines the operational aspects of a dialogue and couples the design of an interface to the functionality of its underlying system

- *a management function* that controls interaction during run time (session tools).

UIMSs are still in their infancy and there is still much discussion about exactly how separate the parts of a system can be. For this reason, some people prefer to see a UIMS as consisting on the one hand of a user interface design environment or UIDE (concerned with the design of icons, screens and dialogue specification) (Foley *et al.*, 1989) and on the other of an interface management system (concerned with runtime facilities).

Just as an AWB serves the need of the system designers, so a UIMS serves the needs of interface designers. At present these tool kits tend to be separate, but increasingly they will come together as system development methodologies (such as SSADM) recognize the importance of user interface design.

Artificial intelligence tool kits

Although artificial intelligence (AI) or expert systems are not as widely used as they might be, their importance is increasingly being recognized. The collection of tools aimed at the production and use of AI systems is known as an AI tool kit. Smaller versions tend to be known as expert system shells. Both of these are expert system development environments.

There are two principal methods of representing knowledge in expert systems: *frames*, which are *objects* consisting of data and procedures, and *rules*, which are procedures of the form *IF premise THEN draw conclusion.* Frames are a particularly powerful representation because they can be arranged into hierarchies with objects lower down the hierarchy automatically inheriting the values and behaviour of objects higher up. All the main AI tool kits support these two methods of knowledge representation by providing appropriate languages and tools. Expert system shells may provide only one of these (usually a rule-based language).

AI tool kits may also support access-oriented programming, data-directed programming and active images and *contexts* or *worlds*. Contexts provide facilities for exploring various alternative, hypothetical situations simultaneously. AI tool kits come with a wide variety of programming and debugging tools and (since they are associated with high-resolution workstations) high-quality graphic input and output with many UIMS facilities such as icon editors and menu handlers.

Almost all AI tool kits are built on top of a LISP programming environment and greatly increase productivity by providing higher-level functions aimed directly at the production of expert systems. However, developers are likely to need a good knowledge of LISP in order to exploit the facilities fully.

5.4   Prototyping

The existence of the tools and environments described in Sections 5.2 and 5.3 has both resulted from and contributed to a significant change in approach to system development. The move away from fixed phases and specifications to iterative design has been facilitated by the ability to create and use software prototypes.

A prototype is a software system that simulates or animates the structure, functionality, operations or representations of another system. A prototype should be cheap to produce and should take only a short time to develop. To emphasize this some authors use the term *rapid* prototype (Hekmatpour and Ince, 1988) or *throw-it-away* prototyping.

A prototype is a software system that:

- actually works, that is, it is not an idea or drawing

- will not have a generalized lifetime: at one end of the spectrum it may be thrown away immediately after use, at the other end it may eventually *evolve* into the final system

- may serve many different purposes

- must be built quickly and cheaply

- is an integral part of an iterative process which also includes modification and evaluation.

A prototype will concentrate on some aspects of an interactive system and ignore others, and may differ from final systems in size, reliability, robustness, completeness, and construction materials.

- *Full prototypes* contain complete functionality but provide less performance than the final system.

- *Horizontal prototypes* demonstrate the operational aspects of a system but do not provide full functionality.

- *Vertical prototypes* contain full functionality but only for a restricted part of a system.

'We've used a computer to prototype the structural strength of the project and I'm afraid the results aren't encouraging.'

Why prototype?

Prototyping is an integral part of iterative design. It is also a highly *participatory* approach. In this approach, the *constant evaluation* of any aspect of a system is central to users developing an understanding of, and confidence in, the new system. Traditionally, involving users in system development, and in interface development in particular, has been fraught with problems:

- Users may lack the ability to imagine the ramifications of design decisions.

- Users have often been unable to comment on technical design documents.

- Providing a complete, consistent and readable representation of such a dynamic aspect of a system as an interface has proved virtually impossible.

Prototypes can overcome these problems because they bring the specification to life. When users interact with something as concrete as a real display their expertise about their working environment will surface.

Prototyping provides a relatively cheap and easy means of testing designs early in a design cycle. Prototypes help designers to make decisions by eliciting information from representative users on all aspects of the system: its structure and functionality, the operation sequences, the required representations and user support needs.

Prototyping methods and tools

There are various kinds of prototype and a range of high-quality software tools to support prototyping. One of the skills of the interface developer lies in choosing tools that are appropriate both for the prototyping method chosen and for the purpose to which the prototype is to be put.

It is not always obvious which type of prototyping is being undertaken. The developer may intend a prototype to be thrown away, but in reality it evolves into the final system. Similarly, a developer may begin an evolutionary prototype which is eventually thrown away and replaced by another system. Table 5.5 shows the various prototype methods that are available and appropriate tools.

Table 5.5 Prototype methods and tools

Prototype method	Description	Useful tool
Requirements animation	Allows possible requirements to be demonstrated in a prototype which can then be assessed by users.	Screen painters are suitable for animating the representational aspects. Data manipulation and other high-level languages are suitable for animating the functional aspects. Authoring languages, menu builders and active images tools prototype operational aspects.

Table 5.5 (cont.)

Prototype method	Description	Useful tool
Rapid (throw-it-away) prototyping	Aims to collect information on requirements and the adequacy of possible designs. Recognizes that requirements are likely to be inaccurate when first specified. The emphasis is on *evaluating* the prototype before discarding it in favour of some other implementation.	Representational requirements and designs can be quickly created using screen painters, forms systems, report generators and menu systems. Hypermedia and VHLL systems are also particularly suitable.
Evolutionary prototyping	Compromise between production and prototyping. The system can cope with change *during* and *after* development. Helps overcome the traditional gap between specification and implementation.	It is important to prototype using the facilities that will eventually be used to implement the final system. Additions and amendments are made to the model following evaluation and the system is regenerated.
Incremental prototyping	The system is built incrementally, one section at a time. Incremental prototyping is based on one overall design.	Re-usable software and highly modular languages can be useful as more pieces are 'bolted on' to gradually produce the final system.

Example

Using a VHLL (Prolog) on a powerful machine may be an effective way of determining the functional requirements of a system that is to be implemented in an efficient language such as C on a less powerful machine.

6.1   What is evaluation?

6.2   When to do evaluation

6.3   Methods, techniques and tools

Analytic evaluation

Expert evaluation

Observational evaluation

Survey evaluation

Experimental evaluation

6.4   Which method and when?

6.5   Two approaches to evaluation: usability engineering and contextual inquiry

6.1 What is evaluation?

Evaluation is concerned with gathering information about the usability or potential usability of a system in order either to improve features within an interface and its supporting material or to assess a completed interface. Without an evaluation process a product reaching consumers would be untried; it would reflect the intentions of its designer but there would be no study of the relationship between design and use. In many cases this would be unacceptable for a range of reasons:

- Statutory safety standards have to be met.
- A detailed understanding of use is needed for product refinement.
- Commercial market forces from rival products mean that general levels of performance need to be achieved.

Depending on circumstances, an evaluation process can be directed at one or all of these points and two main objectives can be identified:

- to determine the effectiveness or potential effectiveness of an interface in use
- to provide a means for suggesting improvements.

Every evaluation takes place within a definite context that includes:

- the experience level of users
- the types of task being undertaken
- the system being used
- the environment in which the study takes place.

6.2 When to do evaluation

Evaluation is closely meshed with design and development and can occur at many different points in the design and development cycle, as can be seen from Figure 6.1 (opposite).

- *Formative evaluation* takes place before implementation in order to influence the product that will be produced.
- *Summative evaluation* takes place after implementation with the aim of testing the proper functioning of the final system.

Quality control is a form of summative evaluation in which a product is reviewed to check that it meets its specification. Testing to check that a product meets the prescribed standards of the International Standards Organization (ISO) (see Section 3.6) is another form of summative evaluation.

6.3 Methods, techniques and tools

An evaluation method is a procedure for collecting relevant data concerning the operation of a user–computer interface and users' attitudes towards it. As a basis for discussion, evaluation methods will be classified into one of five categories.

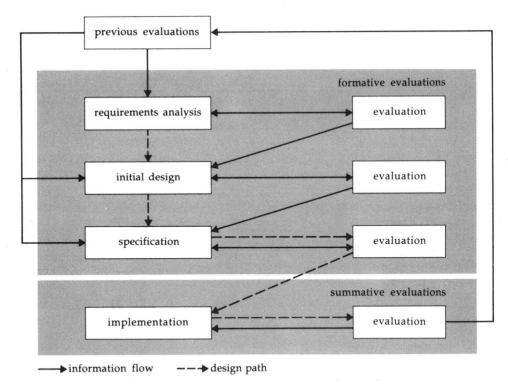

Figure 6.1   Stages of the design cycle in which evaluation may occur

- *Analytic evaluation* uses formal or semi-formal interface descriptions to predict user performance.
- *Expert evaluation* involves experts in assessing an interface.
- *Observational evaluation* involves observing or monitoring users' behaviour while they are using an interface.
- *Survey evaluation* seeks to elicit users' subjective opinions of an interface.
- *Experimental evaluation* uses scientific experimental practice to test hypotheses about the use of an interface.

Analytic evaluation

Analytic evaluation can start early in the design cycle when an interface is represented only by a formal or semi-formal specification. It enables designers to analyse and predict expert performance of error-free tasks in terms of the physical and cognitive operations that must be carried out. In order to do this kind of evaluation it is necessary to derive from the interface specification:

- a *task analysis* (see Section 3.3)
- a *user interface definition*, that is, a document that details the interface operations and gives the input and output sequences for all user–system interactions.

In recent years several analytic evaluation methods have been developed. The differences between these methods revolve around:

- the *task structure*, which can vary from a simple task consisting of a single user command to more complex tasks composed of several commands.

- the *user operations* being evaluated, which can be either simple memory operations closely linked to physical actions or more complex cognitive operations.

The models of user and interface operations used in analytic methods can be either single-layer or multi-layer.

- In *single-layer models* user actions are inserted between separate command input operations, producing a 'flat' representation of an interface in which small cognitive operations punctuate physical operations. One of the most widely known analytic methods is the keystroke-level model (Card *et al.*, 1980) which provides a relatively simple way of analysing expert user performance.

Figure 6.2
single-layer
model

- In contrast, *multi-layer models* use a number of layers to bridge the gap between the high-level operations (the setting of task goals and the selection and ordering of appropriate subtasks) and low-level physical actions, such as command input. Examples of multi-layer models include the GOMS model, cognitive complexity theory (CCT) and command language grammar (CLG), mentioned briefly in Section 3.3.

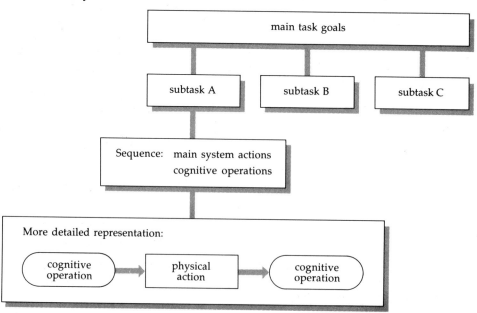

Figure 6.3
multi-layer
model

Other techniques that can be used to analyse how complex an interface is and how easy it should be to learn include the BNF-style grammars of Reisner's interaction language (Reisner, 1981) and task–action grammar (TAG) (Payne and Green, 1986). These are discussed in Section 3.3.

Analytic evaluation methods are attractive because they do not require costly prototypes and user testing. However, these methods should be used with caution because:

- For many applications expert users form a minority and these techniques take no account of learning or error-prone behaviour.
- Apart from the keystroke-level analysis they can be time-consuming and require specialist psychological knowledge.

Expert evaluation

Expert evaluation is a diagnostic method lying between the theoretical approach taken in analytic evaluation and more empirical methods such as observational and experimental evaluation. In expert evaluation, 'experts' (usually people experienced in interface design or human factors research or both) are asked to take the role of less experienced users and describe the potential problems they foresee arising for such users. Expert evaluation that is guided by general 'rules of thumb' is known as heuristic evaluation (Nielsen and Molich, 1990).

This method has certain appeal because it is efficient and provides prescriptive feedback. In particular:

- A small number of experts can usually identify a whole range of potential problems for users during a single session with an interface.
- Often, little prompting is needed to get experts to suggest solutions to the problems identified because they have experienced many interfaces. If they are not involved with the implementation of changes, experts can often propose quite radical changes to an interface. Typical users can suggest solutions to only some of the problems because they do not have enough experience.

It is, however, essential to select experts with caution and give thought to the type of task that they will do. Some points to consider include the following:

- To ensure an impartial opinion the experts should not have been involved with previous versions of the system or prototype under evaluation.
- The experts should have suitable experience.
- The role of the experts needs to be clearly defined to ensure that they adopt the required perspective when using the system.
- The tasks undertaken and the materials given to the experts, such as manuals or tutorials, should be representative of those intended for the eventual users.

Furthermore, the form of reporting adopted by the experts needs consideration so that information is obtained about the most important interface problems. Essentially, one of three styles may be adopted:

- *Structured reporting*. Experts have to report observations in a certain way, for example, the problems encountered, their source, and possible remedies.

- *Unstructured reporting.* Experts report their observations and the common problem areas are then categorized.

- *Predefined categorization.* Experts are given a list of problem categories and they report the occurrence of problems in these categories.

The advantages and disadvantages of these different reporting styles are summarized in Table 6.1.

Table 6.1 Advantages and disadvantages of reporting styles

Reporting style	Advantages	Disadvantages
Structured	Easy to analyse.	Requires time to categorize problems. Inhibits spontaneous suggestions.
Unstructured	Invites spontaneous comments and suggestions.	More difficult to analyse than structured reporting because problems need to be classified.
Predefined categories	Categories of problems already agreed. Very easy to analyse.	Completely inhibits spontaneous comment and advice. May miss problems not already categorized.

Expert evaluation can have considerable appeal because it is usually less costly than methods that involve user testing and because experts often suggest solutions to the problems that they identify. It is, however, important to be aware of the potential drawbacks of expert evaluation:

- Experts are often renowned for their strong views and preferences, in other words, *biases*.

- It is often difficult to find people *experienced* in both a particular type of system application and HCI research.

- Good *role playing* requires an extraordinary amount of information about the knowledge level of the users, their typical tasks and their responses to problems.

- Expert evaluation cannot capture the variety of *real users' behaviour*. Novice users can do some very unexpected things.

Observational evaluation

Observational evaluation involves collecting data that provide information about what users do when they interact with an interface. The observation may be carried out in a location especially selected for the evaluation such as a usability laboratory or informally in a user's normal work environment with minimal interference to the user.

A variety of data collection techniques may be employed:

- *Direct observation* involves observing users during task execution, with the evaluator making notes on user performance and possibly timing sequences of actions. However, direct observation is an obtrusive method because often users are constantly aware that their performance is being monitored, and this can alter their performance levels. (This is known as the *Hawthorne effect*.)

- *Video recording* can be used to record visible aspects of user activity. The recording is then replayed and users' problems are analysed. When users and evaluators work together on the interpretation of protocols, this is known as *participative evaluation* (Wright and Monk, 1989).

'Unfortunately it was after the robbery that we discovered the camera was wrongly positioned.'

- *Software logging* can be used to record the dialogue between user and system. It usually consists of a time-stamped log of user input and system responses. The advantage of this method is that it is unobtrusive. A variant of this technique exists in which the whole interaction is recorded and can then be reproduced for analysis.

- *Interactive observation* is a variant on straightforward observational evaluation which has been termed the 'Wizard of Oz' method (Kelley, 1984). The main feature of this method is that there is a hidden operator who either simulates all the output from the system or amends user input and system output to overcome deficiencies in the system.

- *Verbal protocols* are records of users' spoken observations and thoughts. Video recording is coupled with some form of verbal record, known as a verbal (or think-aloud) protocol, produced by a user while undertaking set tasks. From the protocol a wide range of information can be obtained, for example, the user's planning for the particular task, recall of commands and arguments, and understanding of the command operations, system responses and error situations (Carroll and Mack, 1984). However, users often find it difficult to put their thoughts into words while trying to solve a difficult problem.

- *Variations on verbal protocols* include evaluating the performance of pairs of users (so that prompting is avoided), incorporating question-asking, or obtaining protocols after the tasks have been completed (post-event protocols). In the case of post-event protocols, users view videos of their actions and provide a commentary on what they were trying to do. An obvious problem with this technique is that users may, with hindsight, rationalize their actions. An obvious advantage is that the technique is suitable for use with tasks that are safety-critical, require intense concentration or are time-critical.

The exact form that a subsequent data analysis takes will depend on the aims underlying the evaluation, but two broad categories can be identified:

- *Task-based analysis* attempts to determine how users tackled the tasks given, where the major difficulties lie and what can be done.

- *Performance-based analysis* seeks to obtain clearly defined performance measures from the data collected. The most common measures are: frequency of correct task completion, task timing, use of commands, frequency of user errors, and time required for various cognitive activities such as pausing within and between commands or reading or inspecting various areas of the screen display.

An important factor in the use of different observational methods is the trade-off between time spent and depth of analysis. In-depth analysis can be very time-consuming and a ratio of 5:1 (analysis time to recording/logging time) is often cited.

Survey evaluation

The purpose of survey methods is to address users' subjective opinions through the use of either interviews or questionnaires.

Interviews need careful planning so that the line of questioning followed is relevant to the interface issues being evaluated. Usually, some form of plan is made before the interview: either the sequence of general topics to be covered is determined or some form of checklist of topics or questions is prepared. Whatever type of plan is adopted, the interview can follow either a structured or a flexible style:

- A *structured interview* has a set sequence of predetermined questions and allows no exploration of individual attitudes. This fixed structure is often found in public opinion surveys.

- A *flexible interview* has some set topics but no set sequence, and it develops in response to the interviewees' replies and personal attitudes.

Structured interviews tend to be easier to conduct and considerably easier to analyse than flexible interviews but important details relating to the user's situation may not be recorded.

Questionnaires provide a different approach and broadly speaking there are two types of possible question structure:

- *Open questions* are those where the respondent is free to provide her own answers.

- *Closed questions* ask the respondent to select an answer from a choice of alternative replies.

Open questions provide a rich source of data but may be difficult to analyse. Closed questions are generally easier to analyse than open questions because usually one of the following forms of rating scale is associated with them.

- The simplest rating scales are checklists consisting of basic alternative responses to a very specific question. For example, a three-point scale of 'yes', 'no' and 'don't know' is often used, as shown in Figure 6.4. Checklists are also used to check and record the presence or absence of specific features.

Can you use the following text editing commands?

	yes	no	don't know
DUPLICATE	☐	☐	☐
PASTE	☐	☐	☐

Figure 6.4   A simple checklist

- More complex *multi-point* scales increase the number of points in the rating scales; the meanings of either each individual point or just the end points are given, as shown in Figure 6.5.

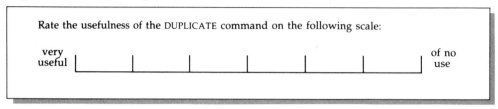

Figure 6.5   An example of a multi-point rating scale

- One variant on the multi-point rating scale is the *Likert scale*, shown in Figure 6.6, where the strength of agreement with a clear statement is measured.

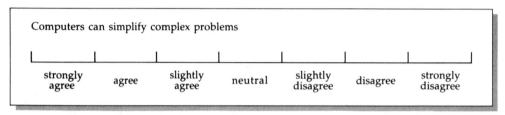

Figure 6.6   An example of a Likert scale

- A popular form of attitude scale used in HCI research is the *semantic differential* scale as shown in Figure 6.7. This scale has bi-polar adjectives (such as easy–difficult, clear–confusing) at the end points, and respondents rate an interface on a scale between these paired adjectives.

Rate the Beauxarts drawing package on the following dimensions:

	extremely	quite	slightly	neutral	slightly	quite	extremely	
easy								difficult
clear								confusing
fun								dreary

Figure 6.7   An example of a semantic differential scale

- Finally, a named scale can be dispensed with and particular items can be placed in a specified number order. For example, items can be ranked for their usefulness, as shown in the part of a *ranked order* questionnaire in Figure 6.8. A rank ordering process is most successful for quite limited groups of items, as large groups can mean that respondents give arbitrary rankings.

Place the following commands in order of usefulness:
(use a scale of 1 to 4 where 1 is the most useful)

PASTE ☐   DUPLICATE ☐   GROUP ☐   CLEAR ☐

Figure 6.8   An example of a ranked order questionnaire

Once questionnaires have been given to a selected population, the responses obtained can be converted into numerical values and a statistical analysis can be performed.

Knowledge elicitation techniques commonly used in expert system development may also be useful for obtaining users' opinions (see Welbank (1990) for further information).

Experimental evaluation

An important feature of the experimental approach is that an evaluator can manipulate a number of factors associated with interface design and study their effects on various aspects of user performance. This approach is based on careful control of an evaluation; before testing, the required level of user experience and the types of manipulation to be made to both tasks and interface features are specified. Usually, the number of factors studied is deliberately limited so that causal relationships can be clearly established.

The planning of an experiment requires the specification of three main elements:

- The purpose of the evaluation has to be expressed in terms of what is being changed, what is being kept constant and what is being measured.
- The hypotheses have to be stated in a way that can be tested.
- Statistical tests have to be selected to check the reliability of the results.

Practical issues also need to be considered, including:

- *procedural* issues such as user preparation
- the *structure* of tasks
- *time* needed to complete the experiment.

Care must also be taken with the results, and issues to consider include:

- possible alternative interpretations of the results
- whether or not the results are generalizable.

It is worth doing a pilot study to determine the suitability of an experimental design before time, effort and money are invested in a full-scale evaluation.

Standard scientific experimental methods are often used in the development and use of interface standards (see Section 3.6).

Performing a well-designed experimental evaluation requires knowledge of scientific experimentation, and readers unfamiliar with experimental methods would be well advised to consult more specialist texts (for example, Robson, 1983).

6.4   Which method and when?

The general differences among the five evaluation methods can be summarized under three categories: the stage of interface development for which they are suitable, the extent and type of user involvement, and the production of either qualitative or quantitative data. Table 6.2 shows the key differences.

Table 6.2   Differences among the five evaluation methods

Method	Interface development	User involvement	Data and information*
Analytic	Specification	No users, tasks specified	Quantitative
Expert	Specification or prototype	Role playing, no task restrictions	Qualitative
Observational	Simulation or prototype	Real users, no task restrictions	Qualitative/ quantitative
Survey	Simulation or prototype	Real users, no task restrictions	Qualitative/ quantitative
Experimental	Normally full prototype	Real users, no task restrictions	Qualitative/ quantitative

* Quantitative data deal with either user performance or attitudes that can be recorded in a numerical form. Qualitative data focus on reports and opinions that may be categorized in some way but are not reduced to numerical values.

A number of advantages and disadvantages have also been identified for each method and these are summarized in Table 6.3.

Table 6.3 Advantages and disadvantages of the evaluation methods

Method	Advantages	Disadvantages
Analytic	Usable early in design. Few resources required, therefore cheap.	Narrow focus. Lack of diagnostic output for redesign. Broad assumptions of users' cognitive operations. Limited guidance on how to use methods, therefore can be difficult for evaluator.

Table 6.3 (cont.)

Method	Advantages	Disadvantages
Expert	Strongly diagnostic. Overview of whole interface. Few resources needed (apart from paying experts), therefore cheap. High potential return (detects significant problems).	Restrictions in role playing. Subject to bias. Problems locating experts. Cannot capture real user behaviour.
Observational	Quickly highlights difficulties. Verbal protocols valuable source of information. Can be used for rapid iterative development. Rich qualitative data.	Observation can affect user activity and performance levels. Analysis of data can be time-consuming and resource-consuming.
Survey	Addresses users' opinions and understanding of interface. Can be made to be diagnostic. Can be applied to users and designers. Questions can be tailored to the individual. Rating scales lead to quantitative results. Can be used on a large group of users.	User experience important. Low response rates (especially to mailed questionnaires). Possible interviewer bias. Possible response bias. Analysis can be complicated and lengthy. Interviews very time-consuming.
Experimental	Powerful method (dependent on the effects investigated). Quantitative data for statistical analysis. Can compare different groups of users. Reliability and validity good. Replicable.	High resource demands. Requires knowledge of experimental method. Time spent on experiments can mean evaluation is difficult to integrate into design cycle. Tasks can be artificial and restricted. Cannot always generalize to full system in typical working situation.

Other factors that need to be considered in the selection of an evaluation method include:

- The exact purpose of the evaluation.

- The external limitations imposed on the evaluation process, such as the time constraints of the development cycle, cost and availability of equipment or expertise.

- Biases in the data collected: how much the evaluation affects the situation being evaluated (known as the ecological validity), the reliability of the methods, and so on.

- Practical questions such as: Are the data easy to gather? How long will it take? How much will it cost? Are appropriate resources available?

- How well particular methods can be assimilated with industrial and commercial practices (for example, expert evaluation and survey methods can be integrated easily whereas observational techniques are more difficult).

6.5 Two approaches to evaluation: usability engineering and contextual inquiry

There are many approaches to doing evaluation. Two that are commonly discussed in the literature are usability engineering and contextual inquiry. The approaches used will influence the choice of method.

Usability engineering is closely integrated with design and it was defined and discussed in Section 3.3; here we consider only the evaluation aspects.

Cycles of 'design–test–redesign' ensure that the product under development attains the usability goals that were quantitatively specified in a *usability specification* (see Section 3.3).

Observational methods are the most commonly used. Video and automatic logging capture users' performance on carefully constructed tasks known as *benchmark tasks*. Questionnaires and interviews are used to collect data about users' opinions.

The observation is often done within the context of a *usability laboratory*, which is a small room with a one-way mirror in one wall so that an evaluator can observe the subject without being seen. While this form of laboratory testing provides valuable information about how users perform the benchmark tasks in a laboratory, it does not always accurately reflect how they use the system in their normal work environments.

Some of the key differences between laboratory conditions and normal work environments (Whiteside *et al.*, 1988) are:

- *Work*. For example, typical word processing benchmark tasks are six pages long, whereas, in practice, working with documents 30 to 50 pages long is not unusual.

- *Time*. Experiments generally have a prescribed time context, whereas in work environments people tend to have more influence on what they do and when they do it.

- *Motivation*. In an experimental context the experimenter controls the situation, whereas usually in the work context there is scope for some negotiation.

- *Social factors*. In the work environment there is normally a social network of support which does not exist in an experimental context.

Contextual inquiry has been developed to obtain information about usability problems experienced by users in their natural working environment. It is based on the premise that users and researchers work collaboratively in a partnership of equality.

The key technique is the *contextual interview* in which a user and researcher discuss the user's goals, way of working and problems encountered when using a system. Any data that are collected, such as video or notes, are then collaboratively analysed by the researcher and user.

'After another week he should be ready to record his first jump.'

Techniques like contextual inquiry are likely to grow in importance with the increase in multimedia systems and collaborative and shared working practices, where laboratory testing is an unrealistic setting.

An excellent overview of the development of usability engineering and contextual inquiry is provided by Whiteside *et al.*, 1988.

The following factors are likely to continue to influence the computing systems of the future:

- faster processing
- greater memory capacity
- greater flexibility of usage
- parallel processors
- high-capacity digital networks
- advanced graphics capabilities
- multimedia
- improved speech recognition and generation
- novel input and output devices
- ease of portability due to reduced size.

The availability of cheap workstations that include CD-ROM in addition to a hard disk will considerably influence the way in which computer systems are used. Multimedia and multi-modal systems are emerging, with text-based systems like HyperCard® giving way to more complex systems in which sound, high-quality graphics, video and videodisk are integrated.

Systems now exist that can combine live digital television, pre-recorded digital video and conventional HyperCard®-type software, and which are thus truly multimedia. Visualization is already important, and we can expect users to be dealing with more graphic representations with less emphasis on textual ones.

In addition, recent developments in telecommunications such as ISDN (integrated services digital network) and high-definition TV are enabling increasingly large amounts and different types of information to be channelled through networks. Images, text and speech will all be transmitted on a single bandwidth with minimum loss of efficiency and quality. Information databases across the world will become much more readily accessible.

Developments in multimedia systems are being accompanied by new input and output devices that enable feet, both hands, eyes, voice and various forms of gesture to be used (see Table 4.4 in Section 4.1). Using some of these devices will make users part of an illusory world in which, for example, they can seem to walk through three-dimensional space or stand in the middle of a squash court waiting to hit a ball rebounding from any of four walls. This phenomenon is known as virtual reality. Already examples exist for playing games, and prototypes are being investigated for other tasks such as flying training for pilots. One of the best-known examples is the dataglove (see Table 4.4 in Section 4.1).

The impact of knowledge-based techniques is likely to increase both with regard to software systems as a whole and HCI in particular. Recently attention has focused on intelligent interface agents which are seen as specialized knowledge-based systems that can act on behalf of the user to provide 'expertise, skill, and labour' (Laurel, 1990) in some aspects of interaction. Negroponte (1989) sees these multiple-agent systems as the wave of the future, providing personalized 'theatrical metaphor' interfaces and dealing with routine tasks so that users are able to concentrate on their central concerns.

Advances in technology will change the way that people live and the kinds of things that they are able to do. For example, people living and working in remote physical locations will be united by technology and able to work collaboratively. Already the advent of small, portable, lap-top computers and modems has changed the way that some people work.

Successful use of this technology will depend upon the identification of:

- the organizational changes that are needed to incorporate multimedia systems, multi-tasking collaborative working practices and other features of advanced technology into work environments
- the development of reliable and easy-to-use interfaces because many users will be unfamiliar with new technology (just as they are with current electronic mail systems).

Understanding these issues in turn requires a better understanding of the perceptual, social and cognitive processes of human–computer interaction. Some questions that will need to be addressed by HCI specialists include:

- What kinds of conceptual model and analogy best represent applications on different media and distributed systems?
- What kinds of tasks and, correspondingly, what kinds of dialogue are most suitable for multimedia and collaborative systems?

'It's harassment in the workplace. This robot keeps reaching over and loosening his neighbour's nuts'

- How can users be helped to focus their attention appropriately on different parts of a system?
- What kinds of navigation aid will help users to find their way through large multimedia systems?
- What kinds of new device are optimal for human spatial and sensori-motor skills?
- How much intelligence can and should intelligent systems contain?

As the capability increases for making interfaces more directly manipulative and realistic, human–computer interaction will change and more advanced psychological theories will be needed to guide design. For example, our understanding of the mental models that people develop and the role of analogy in learning to use multimedia and collaborative systems is very limited. As graphic interfaces become even more complex we shall also need to consider the interpretation of objects in three-dimensional representation much more – a subject which has received only scant attention so far.

Designers will need well-designed methods and tools to capitalize on the technology available while at the same time making sure that it is harnessed to enhance as many people's lives as possible. This means not only being able to understand what is technically possible but also appreciating what is humanly feasible.

At present, good interface design relies heavily on iteration, in which users evaluate various designs and provide feedback, which in turn leads to the improvement of the design. Better prototyping methods, design tools and design environments will facilitate this process, particularly if research in user interface management systems fulfils its promises. There is also a move within HCI to continue to develop more rigorous and formal design methods, in which interface design methodologies integrate with or emulate trends in software engineering design methodologies, such as Jackson (Jackson, 1975), Yourdon (Yourdon and Constantine, 1979) and SSADM (Downes *et al.*, 1989), but are user centred. In particular, we can expect to see more design notations and computerized design tools as part of computer-aided software engineering (CASE) environments which can produce a prototype upon receipt of an appropriately specified design.

Just as visualization will become increasingly important to users, so too will its importance for designers increase. We can expect software development at all stages to deal with graphic representations and not simply textual ones. Although still in the research stage, this is already starting to happen to many aspects of computing. Furthermore, with increasingly sophisticated interfaces comes the need for more supportive design tools. The days when designers were regarded as technical specialists who would cope with poorly designed development tools will end, particularly as the production of third-party multimedia software continues to increase.

Although it is impossible to predict exactly what the future will bring, there is consensus about two things (Weedon, 1992). The first is that technology will continue to change at a phenomenal rate and, consequently, so will the tasks that people do at work, at home and in their leisure time. The second is that HCI research, design and development will play an essential role in technological development and will continue to be a stimulating and vitally important field for the foreseeable future. Designers will have to take HCI considerations into account in order to develop computer systems that are safe, effective, efficient, enjoyable, and hence profitable.

affordance an aspect of an object which makes it obvious how the object is to be used; for example, a panel on a door to indicate 'push' and a vertical handle to indicate 'pull'.

agent a character that initiates action.

analytic evaluation a type of evaluation that uses formal or semi-formal interface descriptions to predict user performance.

anthropology the study of the physical and cultural aspects of humankind.

artificial intelligence (AI) the study of how computers can mimic human thought and the insights this can give about how people think.

auditory output device an output device that uses sound.

Backus–Naur form (BNF) a grammatical notation used to specify programming languages.

benchmark task a standard laboratory task used by many companies in the evaluation of products.

bespoke system a system commissioned by an organization for its own use.

CD-ROM (compact disk – read-only memory) an adaptation of optical read-only compact disks for use with general digital data.

closed question a question in which the respondent is asked to select an answer from a set choice of alternative replies.

cognitive involving the processing of information in the mind.

cognitive modelling the modelling of the cognitive knowledge needed, and the physical actions that a user must carry out, in order to do a task.

cognitive psychology the study of how information is processed and represented in the mind.

command a form of communication with a computer system, usually via a keyboard, in which a request is made for action by inputting a short word or abbreviation.

command language grammar (CLG) an analysis technique based on a grammar that describes the interface at four different, related levels.

communication style see **dialogue**.

computer science the study of the construction of hardware and software, and computer applications.

computer screen an electronically generated visual display, usually a cathode ray tube, plasma, liquid crystal or light-emitting diode display.

computer-supported co-operative working (CSCW) when two or more people work collaboratively supported by computers.

concatenation the artificial production of speech by chaining together pre-recorded units of human speech.

conceptual model see **design model**.

contextual inquiry an evaluation approach in which both users and researchers participate to identify and understand usability problems within the normal working environment of the user.

contextual interview an interview in which the user and researcher discuss user goals, ways of working and problems encountered when using a system.

continuous speech recognition system a system that can recognize key words when they are spoken in a string of other words.

design model the knowledge that a designer has about the system and the way it should work.

dialogue the exchange of instructions and information that takes place between a user and a computer system.

direct manipulation a communication style in which objects are represented on the computer screen as realistically as possible, and can be manipulated by the user in ways analogous to how the user would manipulate the real object; generally actions are reversible.

distributed model a shared model of the system in which parts of the representation are cognitively distributed amongst several people working together.

electro-physiological input a means of input in which eye movement is tracked by implanting electrodes in the eye muscles.

encoding converting information from the environment into some form of internal, mental representation or model.

ergonomics the study of human beings in relationship to their environment, and the engineering of that environment for comfort, efficiency and safety.

evaluation method a procedure for collecting relevant data concerning the operation of a user–computer interface.

evaluation process the gathering of information within a specified context on the usability or potential usability of an interface, and the use of that information either to improve features within the interface and the supporting material or to assess the completed interface.

feedback the response of a system which can be often at a low level, and which indicates either that all is well or that it is not.

fixed menu a 'permanently' visible menu.

flexible interview an interview that has some set topics but no set sequence, and which follows the interviewees' replies and personal attitudes.

form-fill a communication style in which the computer elicits information from the user by presenting a form, analogous to a paper form, to be filled in by the user.

formative evaluation an evaluation that takes place before implementation and which influences the development of the product.

GOMS a task analysis technique which uses goals, operators, methods and selection rules to describe how a set of tasks is to be accomplished.

graphical user interface (GUI) a highly graphical interface with WIMP and direct manipulation characteristics.

hierarchical task analysis (HTA) a method that aims to describe a task in terms of a hierarchy of operations and plans.

human–computer interaction, HCI the study of how human beings interact with computers.

hypermedia virtual media in which information is held in a network of nodes, which may have links to other nodes, and where users can decide how much of the information they want to see.

hypertext similar to hypermedia except that hypertext contains only text with diagrams.

impact analysis a form of ranking, used to rank user problems in order of their individual contribution to the total problem time.

information technology (IT) the processing and transfer of information using technology, in particular computers.

input device any device that transfers information from the outside world into an electronic form that the computer can use.

interaction the exchange that occurs between users and computers.

isolated word recognition system a system that can understand key words when they are spoken in isolation from other words.

ISDN (integrated services digital network) telecommunications network on which images, text and speech can be transmitted on the same bandwidth.

Likert scale a rating scale in which the strength of agreement with a clear statement is measured.

man–machine interface, MMI an older term for human–computer interaction; it referred to many semi-automatic and automatic machines.

media tool sets up input and output structures, linking them to low-level objects such as buttons and pop-up menus.

mental model a mental representation that a person uses to organize her experience of herself, others, the environment and the things with which she interacts.

menu a set of options displayed on a screen where the selection and execution of one (or more) of the options results in a change in the state of the interface.

microform a form of output in which text, and sometimes graphics, are reduced greatly in size and recorded on film. Includes microfiche and microfilm.

multi-layer model a model of an interface that uses a number of layers to bridge the gap between the high-level operations (the setting of task goals and the selection and ordering of the appropriate subtasks) and the low-level physical actions, such as command input.

multimedia an umbrella term for the integration of different media such as text, graphics, video, still photographs and sound in a single application.

multitasking switching between several different tasks at the interface.

open question a question in which the respondent is free to provide her own answer.

organizational psychology the study of the varying structures, cultures and working practices of organizations and their influence on human behaviour and relationships at work.

output device any device which takes the internal, electronic representation from within a computer and makes it available in the outside world, in electronic, electrical or any other perceptible form.

participative design a method involving users that deals with a whole system, taking social and organizational requirements into account at an early stage in the development cycle.

philosophy one of the disciplines contributing to HCI, where it is primarily concerned with the impact of and ethics surrounding the introduction of IT into the world.

photoelectric reflection a means of tracking eye movement by recording reflection from the eye.

pop-up menu a menu that appears when the user clicks on a particular part of a display.

printer a device for displaying text on paper output.

production rule a formal rule of the form IF (*premise*) THEN (*conclusion*), to define how to produce a correct statement in a programming language; used in BNF.

psychology the study of human behaviour; psychology, and particularly its branch 'cognitive psychology', have contributed to HCI.

pull-down menu a menu that 'pulls down' like a roller blind from a title bar at the top of a display.

qualitative data data that may be categorized in some way but are not reduced to numerical values.

quantitative data data that can be recorded in a numerical form.

question and answer dialogue a communication style in which the computer (usually) initiates questions and the user enters yes/no or menu choices.

ranked order scale a scale that provides a way of ranking items for their usefulness.

requirements analysis an investigation to specify what the system should do (that is, the system's functionality).

selective attention the ability to take notice of one particular item of information from amongst a mass of items competing for one's attention.

semantic differential scale a scale with bi-polar adjectives (such as easy–difficult, clear–confusing) at its end points; respondents rate an interface on a scale between these paired adjectives.

session tool a management function controlling actual interaction.

single-layer model a model of an interface that produces a 'flat' representation in which small cognitive operations punctuate physical operations.

social psychology the study of human behaviour and relationships within differing social groups, and the characteristics of those groups that affect the individuals within them.

sociology the study of social groups and their dynamics; it has contributed to HCI.

software engineering a formal approach to the construction of computer software.

speaker-dependent system a speech-recognition system that must be 'trained' to recognize one user's voice.

speaker-independent system a speech-recognition system that can recognize words spoken by most people, regardless of differences in pitch, tone, accent, and so on.

spreadsheet a communication style analogous to an accountant's spreadsheet, but in which many functions, such as totalling rows or columns, are automated or programmable.

structured design methods software design methods that formalize the processes involved in the phases of software development, using notations.

structured interview an interview that has predetermined questions and a set sequence of questions, and allows no exploration of individual attitudes.

subtask a part of a larger task; in system design, a task must be broken down into subtasks that are small enough to be converted to a dialogue with the computer system.

summative evaluation any evaluation that takes place after implementation.

synthesis-by-rule the artificial production of speech through the use of rules of pronunciation, intonation and physical characteristics of human speech.

system image the image a system conveys to the user by its interface, behaviour and documentation, and which should form the basis of the user's mental model of the system.

system specification an initial statement of a customer's requirements produced by software engineers.

tactile output device an output device that uses the user's sense of touch, e.g. Braille screen readers.

task an activity that a user of a computer system needs to do in order to achieve an objective.

task analysis any of a variety of forms of analysis of how people work; involves analysing what tasks and subtasks must be done, and how they must be done, in order to achieve required objectives.

task analysis for knowledge-based descriptions (TAKD) a task analysis method in which tasks are described in terms of the knowledge needed to do them.

task–action grammar (TAG) a task analysis method that uses a formal grammar, similar to BNF, to describe users' tasks.

transition diagrams graphic structures indicating states and transitions from one state to another.

usability a measure of the ease with which a system can be learned or used, its safety, effectiveness and efficiency, and the attitude of its users towards it.

usability engineering an approach to system design in which the usability level of a system is specified quantitatively in advance, using metrics.

usability laboratory a small room where a subject performs tasks; it incorporates a one-way mirror in one wall so that an evaluator can observe the subject without being seen.

usability metrics the measures that are collected for describing the usability of a system.

usability specification the document that guides design by specifying usability metrics and tests. It defines the acceptable performance of the system for particular users and tasks.

usability testing assessment of the usability of a system, in terms of learnability, ease of use, flexibility, safety, effectiveness, efficiency and the attitude of users to the system.

user interface all the aspects of a computer system of which the user is aware and which the user uses to communicate with the system.

user models cognitive and performance models of the user which have been developed as design and evaluation tools.

user–system interaction (USI) A similar term to, but more general than, HCI. (See **human–computer interaction**.)

virtual reality a state in which the user has the illusion of being in a three-dimensional world created by the computer system.

visual output device any output device that uses the user's sense of sight (visual display unit); screens and paper output are the most common, although video is becoming available.

window a restricted view of data on a VDU, particularly when the VDU screen can have more than one window active, each with a different view.

The symbols (T) and (E) are included after some references to indicate their nature. (T) = Technical; (E) = Easy. Articles without (T) or (E) can be considered as intermediate.

APEX (1979) Office technology – the trade union response, quoted in JONES, T. (ed.) (1980) Microelectronics and Society, The Open University Press, Milton Keynes.

APPLE COMPUTER, INC. (1987) Inside Macintosh, Addison–Wesley, Wokingham. (T)

BJØRN-ANDERSEN, N. (1986) Understanding the nature of the office for the design of third wave offices, in HARRISON, M. D. and MONK, A. F. (eds) People and Computers: Designing for Usability: Proceedings of the BCS HCI Specialist Group, Cambridge University Press, Cambridge.

BOOTH, P. (1989) An Introduction to Human–Computer Interaction, Lawrence Erlbaum Associates, Hove.

CAMPBELL, I. (1987) Standardization, availability and use of PCTE, Information and Software Technology, Vol. 29, no. 8, pp. 411–4. (T)

CARD, S. K., ENGLISH, W. K. and BURR, B. J. (1978) Evaluation of mouse, rate-controlled isometric joystick, step keys, and text keys for text selection on a CRT, Ergonomics, Vol. 21, no. 8, pp. 601–13. (T)

CARD, S. K., MORAN, T. P. and NEWELL, A. (1980) The keystroke-level model for user performance time with interactive systems, Communications of the ACM, Vol. 23, no. 7, pp. 396–410. Reprinted as Chapter 16 in PREECE, J. and KELLER, L. (eds) (1990) pp. 327–56. (T)

CARD, S. K., MORAN, T. P. and NEWELL, A. (1983) The Psychology of Human–Computer Interaction, Lawrence Erlbaum Associates, Hillsdale, New Jersey. (T)

CARROLL, J. M. (1990) The Nurnberg Funnel: Designing Minimalist Instruction for Practical Computer Skills, MIT Press, Cambridge, Massachusetts.

CARROLL, J. M. and MACK, R. L. (1984) Learning to use a word processor: by doing, by thinking, and by knowing, in THOMAS, J. C. and SCHNEIDER, M. L. (eds) Human Factors in Computer Systems, Ablex, Norwood, New Jersey, pp. 13–51.

CARROLL, J. M. and RAY, A. S. (1988) Prompting, feedback and error correction on the design of a scenario machine, International Journal of Man–Machine Studies, Vol. 28, no. 1, pp 11–27.

CARROLL, J. M., MACK, R. L. and KELLOGG, W. A. (1988a) Interface metaphors and design, in HELANDER, M. (ed.) (1988) pp. 67–85.

CARROLL, J. M., SMITH-KERKER, P. L., FORD, J. R. and MAZUR-RIMETZ, S. A. (1988b) The Minimal Manual, Human–Computer Interaction, Vol. 3, pp. 123–53.

CARROLL, J. M., MACK, R. L., LEWIS, C., GRISCHKOWSKI, N. and ROBERTSON, S. (1985) Exploring a word processor, Human–Computer Interaction, Vol. 1, pp. 283–307.

CHRIST, R. E. (1975) Review and analysis of colour coding research for visual displays, Human Factors, Vol. 17, no. 6, pp. 542–70.

CZAJA, S. J., HAMMOND, K., BLASCOVICH, J. J. and SWEDE, H. (1986) Learning to use a word-processing system as a function of training strategy, *Behaviour and Information Technology*, Vol. 5, pp. 203–16.

DIAPER, D. (1989) (ed.) *Task Analysis for Human–Computer Interaction*, Ellis Horwood, Chichester.

DONEY, A. and SETON, J. (1988) Using colour, in RUBIN, T. (ed.) *User Interface Design for Computer Systems*, Ellis Horwood, Chichester.

DOWNES, E., CLARE, P. and COE, I. (1991) *Structured Systems Analysis and Design Method: Application and Context*, Prentice Hall, New York.

EASON, K. D. (1988) *Information Technology and Organizational Change*, Taylor and Francis, London. (E)

EASON, K. D. and HARKER, S. (1980) *An Open Systems Approach to Task Analysis*, Internal Report, HUSAT Research Centre, Loughborough University of Technology.

ELKERTON, J. (1988) Online aiding for human–computer interfaces, in HELANDER, M. (ed.) (1988) pp. 345–64. (T)

FOLEY, J., KIM, W. C., KOVACEVIC, S. and MURRAY, K. (1989) Defining interfaces at a high level of abstraction, *IEEE Software*, Jan., pp. 25–32.

FOLEY, J. D., McCORMIK, K. and BLESER, T. (1982) Documenting the design of user–computer interfaces in an industrial course, *Workstation User Interface Design, Vols. 1 and 2*, organized by the Alvey Directorate of the Department of Trade and Industry, copyright Computer Graphics Consultants, Inc., Washington, DC.

FURNAS, G. W. (1991) New graphical reasoning models for understanding graphical interfaces, in ROBERTSON, S. P., OLSON, G. M. and OLSON, J. S. (eds) *Reaching Through Technology*, CHI '91 Conference Proceedings, ACM Press, New York, pp. 71–8. (T)

GAINES, B. R. and SHAW, M. L. G. (1984) *The Art of Computer Conversation: A New Medium for Communication*, Prentice Hall, Englewood Cliffs, New Jersey.

GOULD, J. D. and LEWIS, C. (1985) Designing for usability: key principles and what designers think, *Communications of the ACM*, Vol. 28, no. 3, pp. 300–11. (T)

HEKMATPOUR, S. and INCE, D. (1988) *Software Prototyping, Formal Methods and VDM*, Addison–Wesley, Wokingham. (T)

HELANDER, M. (ed.) (1988) *Handbook of Human–Computer Interaction*, North–Holland, Amsterdam. (Generally T)

HILGARD, E. R., ATKINSON, R. L. and ATKINSON, R. C. (1979) *Introduction to Psychology*, 7th edn, Harcourt Brace Jovanovich, London.

INTERNATIONAL STANDARDS ORGANIZATION (1985) *Information Processing System – Computer Graphics – Graphical Kernel System (GKS) Functional Description*, ISO 7942. Also published as BS6390: 1985.

JACKSON, M. (1975) *Principles of Program Design*, Academic Press, London. (T)

JOHNSON, J., DIAPER, D. and LONG, J. (1985) Tasks, skills and knowledge: task analysis for knowledge based descriptions, in SHACKEL, B. (ed.), *Human–Computer Interaction*, Elsevier Science Publishers B. V. (North-Holland), pp. 499–503. (T)

KELLEY, J. F. (1984) An iterative design methodology for user-friendly natural language office information applications, *ACM Transactions on Office Information Systems*, Vol. 2, pp. 26–41.

KIERAS, D. E. (1988) Towards a practical GOMS model methodology for user interface design, in HELANDER, M. (ed.) (1988), Chapter 7, pp. 135–57. (T)

KIERAS, D. and POLSON, P. G. (1985) An approach to the formal analysis of user complexity, *International Journal of Man–Machine Studies*, Vol. 22, pp. 365–94. (T)

KLOSTER, G. V. and ZELLWEGER, A. (1987) Engineering the man–machine interface for air traffic control, *IEEE Computer*, Vol. 30, no. 9, pp. 47–62. (T)

LAUREL, B. (1990) Interface agents, in LAUREL, B. (ed.), *The Art of Human–Computer Interface Design*, Addison–Wesley, Wokingham.

LEWIS, C. and NORMAN, D. (1986) Designing for error, in NORMAN, D. and DRAPER, S. (eds) *User-Centered System Design*, pp. 411–32, Lawrence Erlbaum Associates, Hillsdale, New Jersey and London.

MACCAULAY, L., FOWLER, C., KIRBY, M. and HUTT, A. (1990) USTM: a new approach to requirements specification, *Interacting with Computers*, Vol. 2, no. 1, pp. 92–108.

MACK, R. L., LEWIS, C. H. and CARROLL, J. M. (1983) Learning to use a word processor: problems and prospects, *ACM Transactions on Office Information Systems*, Vol. 3, July, pp. 254–71. Reprinted as Chapter 8 in PREECE, J. and KELLER, L. (eds) (1990) pp. 185–204.

MARTIN, J. (1986) *Information Engineering, Vols 1 and 2*, Savant, Lancaster.

MILLER, G. A. (1956) The magic number seven plus or minus two: some limits of our capacity for information processing, *Psychological Review*, Vol. 63, no. 2, pp. 81–7.

MORAN, T. P. (1981) The command language grammar, *International Journal of Man–Machine Studies*, Vol. 15, pp. 3–50. (T)

MUMFORD, E. (1983) *Designing Participatively*, Manchester Business School Publications, Manchester. (E)

NEGROPONTE, N. (1989) An iconoclastic view: beyond the desktop metaphor, *International Journal of HCI*, Vol. 1, no. 1, pp. 109–113.

NIELSEN, J. and MOLICH, R. (1990) Heuristic evaluation of user interfaces, in CHEW, J. C. and WHITESIDE, J. (eds) *Empowering People*, CHI '90 Conference Proceedings, ACM Press, New York, pp. 249–56.

NORMAN, D. A. (1988) *The Psychology of Everyday Things*, Basic Books, New York. (E)

NORMAN, D. A. and DRAPER, S. W. (eds) (1986) *User Centred System Design: New Perspectives on Human–Computer Interaction*, Lawrence Erlbaum Associates, Hillsdale, New Jersey.

OBORNE, D. J. (1985) *Computers at Work: A Behavioural Approach*, Wiley, Chichester.

PAPERT, S. (1980) *Mindstorms: Children, Computers and Powerful Ideas*, Harvester Studies in Cognitive Studies 14, Harvester, Brighton. (E)

PAYNE, S. J. and GREEN, T. R. G. (1986) Task–action grammars: a model of the mental representation of task languages, *Human–Computer Interaction*, Vol. 2, no. 2, pp. 93–133. (T)

PCTE Functional Specifications (1986) Bull, GEC, ICL, Olivetti, Nixdorf, Siemens. (T)

PERLMAN, G. (1988) Software tools for user interface development, in HELANDER, M. (ed.) (1988) pp. 819–33. (T)

PHILIPS, M. P., BASHINSKI, H. S., AMMERMAN, H. and FLIGG, C. (1988) A task analytic approach to dialogue design, in HELANDER, M. (ed.) (1988), pp. 835–57. (T)

POLSON, P. G. and KIERAS, D. E (1985) A quantitative model of the learning and performance of text editing knowledge, *CHI '85*, Association for Computing Machinery, New York, pp. 207–12. Reprinted as Chapter 14 in PREECE and KELLER (eds) (1990) pp. 296–307. (T)

PREECE, J. and KELLER, L. (eds) (1990) *Human–Computer Interaction: Selected Readings*, Prentice Hall, London. (Generally T)

REISNER, P. (1981) Formal grammar and human factors design of an interactive system, *IEEE Transactions on Software Engineering*, Vol. SE–7, no. 2, pp. 229–40. (T)

ROBSON, C. (1983) *Experimental Design and Statistics in Psychology*, Penguin, Aylesbury, Bucks., UK. An edited version is printed as Chapter 17 in PREECE, J. and KELLER, L. (eds) (1990) pp. 357–67. (E)

ROGERS, Y. (1989) Icons at the interface: their usefulness, *Interacting with Computers*, Vol. 1, pp. 105–18. (E)

RUBINSTEIN, R. and HERSH, H. (1984) *The Human Factor: Designing Computer Systems for People*, Digital Press, Burlington, Massachusetts. (E)

SCHEIFLER, R. W., GETTYS, J. and NEWMAN, R. (1988) *The X Window System*, Digital Press, Bedford, Massachusetts. (T)

SCHIFF, W. (1980) *Perception: An Applied Approach*, Houghton Mifflin Company, Boston, Massachusetts.

SEBILLOTTE, S. (1988) Hierarchical planning as a method for task analysis: the example of office task analysis, *Behaviour and Information Technology*, Vol. 7, no. 3, pp. 275–93. (T)

SHACKEL, B. (1990) Human factors and usability, in PREECE, J. and KELLER, L. (eds) (1990) Chapter 2, pp. 27–41. (E)

SHNEIDERMAN, B. (1983) Direct manipulation: a step beyond programming languages, *IEEE Computer*, Vol. 16, no. 8, pp. 57–69.

SHNEIDERMAN, B. (1987) *Designing the User Interface: Strategies for Effective Human–Computer Interaction*, Addison–Wesley, Reading, Massachusetts. (2nd ed., 1992) (E)

SMITH, S. L., and MOSIER, J. N. (1986) *Guidelines for Designing User Interface Software, Technical Report ESD-TR-86-27*, USAF Electronic Systems Division, Hanscom Air Force Base, Massachusetts. (T)

STEWART, T. (1991) *Directory of HCI Standards, DTI and Systems Concepts*, Department of Trade and Industry, London.

STRASSMAN, P. A. (1985) *Information Payoff*, The Free Press, New York.

SUCHMAN, L. (1987) *Plans and Situated Actions: The Problem of Human–Machine Communication*, Cambridge University Press, New York.

SUTCLIFFE, A. (1989) Task analysis, systems analysis and design: symbiosis or synthesis? *Interacting with Computers: the Interdisciplinary Journal of Human–Computer Interaction*, Vol. 1, no. 1, pp. 6–12. (T)

TAYLOR, M. E., VINCENT, A. T. and CHILD, D. A. (1990) *Alternatives to Print for Visually Impaired Students: Feasibility Project Report*, unpublished internal report at The Open University, Milton Keynes.

TULLIS, T. S. (1988) Screen design, in HELANDER, M. (ed.) (1988) pp. 377–411. (T)

WARD, F. (1989) Images for the computer age, *National Geographic*, Vol. 175, no. 6, pp. 719–51.

WASSERMAN, A. I. and SHEWMAKE, D. T. (1985) The role of prototypes in the user software engineering (USE) methodology, in HARTSON, H. R. (ed.) *Advances in Human–Computer Interaction*, Ablex Publishing Corp., New Jersey, pp. 191–209. Reprinted as Chapter 19 in PREECE and KELLER (eds) (1990) pp. 385–401. (T)

WATERWORTH, J. A. (1988) *Speech and Language Based Interaction with Machines*, Ellis Horwood, Chichester.

WEEDON, R. A. (1992) *Proceedings of the Conference Computing Curricula for the 1990s*, Computing Department Technical Report 92/10, The Open University, Milton Keynes.

WEINER, M. (1990) The art of finding fault, *Workstation Magazine*, April 1990, pp. 44–47.

WELBANK, M. (1990) An overview of knowledge acquisition methods, *Interacting with Computers*, Vol. 2, no. 1, pp. 83–91. (E)

WHITESIDE, J., BENNETT, J. and HOLTZBLATT, K. (1988) Usability engineering: our experience and evolution, in HELANDER, M. (ed.) (1988), pp. 791–817.

WRIGHT, P. (1980) Usability: the criterion for designing written information, in KOLERS, P. A., WROLSTAD, M. E. and BOUMA, H. (eds), *Processing of Visible Language*, Vol. 2, Plenum Press, New York, pp. 183–206.

WRIGHT, P. and MONK, A. F. (1989) Evaluation for design, in SUTCLIFFE, A. and MACAULAY L. (eds) *People and Computers V. Proceedings of the Fifth Conference of the British Computer Society on Human–Computer Interaction*, Cambridge University Press, pp. 345–58.

YOURDON, E. and CONSTANTINE, L. (1979) *Structured Design*, Prentice Hall, Englewood Cliffs, New Jersey. (T)

Aldus SuperCard® is a registered trademark of Aldus Corporation.

Apple®, HyperCard® and MacPaint® are registered trademarks of Apple Computer Inc.; HyperTalk™, Macintosh™, MacTools™ and QuickTime™ are trademarks of Apple Computer Inc.

GEM® is a registered trademark of Digital Research Inc.

InterPro™ is a trademark of Unisys Corporation.

Microsoft® and MS-DOS® are registered trademarks of Microsoft Inc.

SmallTalk-80™ is a trademark of the Xerox Corporation.

Unix® is a registered trademark of American Telephone and Telegraph Co. Inc.

Grateful acknowledgement is made to the following sources for permission to reproduce copyright material:

Figures

Figures 2.1, 4.4, 4.5: Tullis, T.S. from *Handbook of Human–Computer Interaction*, Helander, M. (ed.), Elsevier Science Publishers; *Figure 2.2*: Rogers, Y., *Interacting with Computers*, Vol. 1, no. 1, Butterworth and Co. (Publishers) Ltd, 1989; *Figures 2.5, 2.6, 2.8, 3.2*: Eason, K., *Informational Technology and Organisational Change*, Taylor & Francis, London, 1988; *Figure 2.7*: Bjørn-Andersen from *People and Computers: Designing for Usability*, Harrison, M.D. and Monk, A.F. (eds), Cambridge University Press, 1986; *Figure 3.3*: Perlman, G. from *Handbook of Human–Computer Interaction*, Helander, M. (ed.), Elsevier Science Publishers; *Figure 3.5*: Card, S.K., Moran, P., Newell, A., *The Psychology of Human–Computer Interaction*, Lawrence Erlbaum Associates, New Jersey, 1983, copyright © 1983 by Lawrence Erlbaum Associates, Inc.; *Figure 3.6*: Foley, J.D. *et al.* from *Workstation User Interface Design*, Sibert, J. (ed.), Computer Graphics Consultants, Inc., 1984; *Figure 3.7*: Sutcliffe, A., adapted from 'Task analysis, systems analysis and design: symbiosis or synthesis', *Journal of Human–Computer Interaction*, Vol. 1, 1989, Butterworth and Co. (Publishers) Ltd, 1989; *Figure 4.1*: Norman, D. from *The Psychology of Everyday Things*, copyright © 1988 by Donald A. Norman. Reprinted by permission of Basic Books, Inc., Publishers, New York; *Figure 4.2*: redrawn from a photograph by Fred Ward, © 1990; *Figure 4.3*: Footmouse, courtesy of Versatron Corporation, Healdsburg, California; *Figures 4.6, 4.8, 4.10, 4.11*: Courtesy of Apple Computer UK; *Figure 4.9*: Shneiderman, B., *Designing the User Interface*, copyright ©1986 Addison-Wesley Publishing Co. Inc., Reading, Massachusetts. Adapted from Fig 3.11 on page 123. Reprinted with permission of the publisher.

Tables

Table 3.1: Whiteside, J., Bennett, J., Holtzblatt, K. from *Handbook of Human–Computer Interaction*, Helander, M. (ed.) Elsevier Science Publishers; *Table 4.9*: Tullis, T.S. from *Handbook of Human–Computer Interaction*, Helander, M. (ed.), Elsevier Science Publishers.

Illustrations

pp. 14, 44, 89, 99, 104, 113, 114, 121: Honeysett, M. (1982) *Microphobia*, Century Hutchinson Ltd, copyright © Martin Honeysett, 1982; *p. 15*: Knight, P. from *The Psychology of Everyday Things*, Chapter 7, Basic Books Inc., Publisher, New York, copyright © Peter Knight; *pp. 17, 39, 43, 47, 49, 54, 58, 69, 81, 84, 123, 125*: Dedini, E., *A Much Much Better World*, Microsoft Press, 1985, copyright © Eldon Dedini; *pp. 22, 32*: drawings by Koren, E., copyright © 1967, 1969, The New Yorker Magazine, Inc.; *p. 27*: Harris, S. from *Introduction to Psychology* published by Harcourt Brace Jovanovich Inc., copyright © Sidney Harris; *p. 28*: Breathed, B. (1989) 'Bloom County', *Guardian*, 21 April 1989, copyright © 1989 Washington Post Co.